WORLD CHRISTIAN BOOKS NO. 9

FROM BRAHMA TO CHRIST

World Christian Books

A SERIES OF BOOKS COVERING THE WHOLE RANGE
OF THE CHRISTIAN FAITH IN THE MODERN WORLD

Edited by Bishop Stephen Neill

*Sponsored by the International Missionary Council
in co-operation with the Christian Literature Council
of Great Britain and the Committee on World
Literacy and Christian Literature of the United
States, and the Department of Overseas Missions of
the Canadian Council of Churches. Published by the
United Society for Christian Literature and the
Lutterworth Press, London.*

WORLD CHRISTIAN BOOKS

No. 9

FROM BRAHMA TO CHRIST

The Story of Narayan Vaman Tilak
and
Lakshmibai his wife

by

LAKSHMIBAI TILAK

UNITED SOCIETY FOR CHRISTIAN LITERATURE

LUTTERWORTH PRESS

London

First published 1956

Second impression 1956

92
T45b
1956

155683

Printed in Great Britain by Page Bros. (Norwich) Ltd.
Mile Cross Lane, Norwich

Preface by the General Editor

The beginning of the twentieth century was a period of hope for the Christian Church. The western Churches appeared strong and rich, and great new Churches were growing quickly in almost all parts of the world. It seemed that the Gospel might spread through the whole earth without meeting serious opposition. Fifty years later all is changed. Every Christian knows that these are hard days for the Church. The old faiths are taking on new life and new power of resistance to the Gospel. New faiths, such as Communism, are attracting millions of believers. Christians are convinced that Jesus Christ is the last Word of God to man, and that all the future is in His hands; but they know also that the Faith cannot survive and grow unless Churches and individuals receive new life, new confidence and new power to witness. In these days every Christian must be an evangelist.

To-day it is not enough to believe—it is necessary also to understand. From every part of the world comes the demand for books that will help the Christian to understand his faith, to find the answers to the questions that he and other men are asking, and to know how to present the Faith to others. The series *World Christian Books* is planned to help in this particular area of Christian need. The books are directed in the first place to the "younger Churches", but the old distinction between younger and older Churches no longer really holds. All Churches are faced by the same problems. In all countries the same questions are being asked. The series is specially planned for those who are called to preach and teach, in the hope that the materials given in these books may help them to carry out their task more effectively. But the aim has also been to write so simply that ordinary members of the Church who wish to study their Faith may be able to use these books as individuals or in study groups and so to grow in knowledge and understanding.

The books are being published first in English, but it is intended that as soon as possible they should be made available in the main languages of the Christian world. Writers have been chosen from various countries and various branches of the Church, with special emphasis on the younger Churches. This means that there will be a variety of voices, but the aim and the hope is that through many minds and many tongues the faith of the Church in its one Lord may be clearly set forth.

STEPHEN NEILL,
Bishop

CONTENTS

EDITORIAL NOTE

The biographical material in this book is drawn from *I Follow After*, the autobiography of Lakshmibai Tilak, published by the Oxford University Press in 1950. The Editor and Publishers of *From Brahma to Christ* desire to express their thanks to the Oxford University Press for permission to use this material.

The translations of poems of Narayan Vaman Tilak at the end of the volume are reproduced, by permission, from a collection published under the title *Bhakti Niranjana* (Flame of Devotion), by his son Mr. D. N. Tilak at the Nagarik Press, Agra Road, Nasik.

The work of selection and editing has been carried out by Canon R. P. Stacy Waddy, formerly a missionary in Western India, and now Warden of the College of the Ascension, Selly Oak, Birmingham. The introduction has also been written by Canon Waddy.

INTRODUCTION

The name of Narayan Vaman Tilak is stamped upon the life and worship of the Christian Church in Western India. He was a true poet, a lover of words and music. He was a true patriot, who wanted his songs and hymns to be on the lips of his people in their own language, and his thoughts and teaching in their hearts. He was a true Christian, and his hymns hold their place in Christian affections because they repeat and convey the truths of the Gospel.

As a Christian poet writing in the Marathi language, Tilak stands by himself. When he was baptized, the Indian Christian hymn-books were full of missionary translations of familiar English hymns. He was the first to bring the genius of a Marathi poet into the service of Christ. Thus did Christian worship begin to become *swadeshi*, racy of the soil and natural to the Indian devotee.

But as a Christian patriot he made as notable a contribution to Indian Church history. "It is possible to say," wrote his wife forty years later, "that the course of thought of the Christian community was changed from the day of Tilak's baptism." He insisted on being baptized by a fellow-countryman and not by any missionary, although he was on terms of closest friendship with Dr. Hume and Dr. Abbott of the American Marathi Mission; and did so not for personal reasons but because of his intense patriotism. This love of his own land and people inspired him with a passionate longing for the day when the fulness of India's rich contribution to Christian worship and understanding should be laid at the feet of Christ.

So he was outspoken in deploring the dependence of his fellow-Christians on missionary leadership and money, and in criticizing those missionaries who seemed content that this should be so. This outspokenness, and the impulsive actions which went with it, cannot have made him an easy colleague, any more than he can ever have been an easy husband. But he was friend as well as goad to the missionaries of the Congregational Church with whom his loyalty was linked.

Certainly he was never in danger of becoming westernized in his new-found faith, as it was easy and natural for others to be. He was a genuine "character", typical of no one but himself, with a deep love of truth and a determined obstinacy in following where it led; a mind ever eager for experiment, matched with a generous heart and reckless courage. It does scant justice to such men to produce a biography. Tilak is fortunate in living on within the pages of his wife's reminiscences, pictures which stood out in her memory as she looked back over the adventures which they had shared.

These selections from her writings set out to tell the story of a family. She is as interested in herself as in her husband, and she reveals not a "great" man but a real man. Still he has power to move, and inspire, and infuriate, and challenge. The pattern is untidy, but so was the man. She makes us laugh with her, at herself and at him; but through the fun we grow in respect for both of them, as they grew in grace and spiritual stature. For Tilak, once freed from the bonds of caste, found in Christianity the soil in which his irresponsible nature grew to spiritual maturity in holiness and humility; and his wife deserves the brave and breathless title *I Follow After* which was given to her account of him.

It is not easy for others to realize the Himalayan difficulty of a Brahman's mind opening to new light, and of his breaking out of the prison cell of caste pride into the world of Christian freedom. In that world many of his fellow-Christians will be of outcaste origin, with little education and no cultural background. This book tells part of the story; it cannot tell the whole history of the Holy Spirit's work of grace in Tilak. His whole-hearted surrender to Christ, and the remarkable influence which he exercised in the later years of his life, must be understood by those who would appreciate his place in the story of the Church.

By his hymns and by his character, Tilak paved the way for that necessary step in the growth of an indigenous Church, when "the Mission" gives way to the Church. Great changes have marked the thirty-five years since his death, and the Indian Church has "followed after" where he explored and pointed the way. He would be glad—and he would still be in a hurry.

The scene of this story is Maharashtra, that part of Western India which fans out from Bombay across the Deccan plain into the Central Provinces. Of the towns mentioned in this book, Jalalpur and Nasik are to the north; Rahuri, Ahmadnagar and Poona to the west; Mahabaleshwar, Satara and Pandharpur to the south; Rajnandgaon is further inland in the Central Provinces, 600 miles from Bombay.

This is the Maratha country, whose mother tongue is Marathi. The language is derived from Sanskrit, the literary language of ancient India, in which the sacred Scriptures of Hinduism are written. Marathi is a

11

vigorous language with a notable literature of its own; the colloquial language borrows freely from Hindi, but literary writers and orators decorate and enrich their vocabulary from Sanskrit literature.

The Aryan invaders of 1500 B.C. or earlier drove the original Dravidian peoples down into South India when they settled into possession of the land. They established their social caste system with its four main divisions: the Brahmans or priests; the nobles and fighting men; the middle classes; and the Sudras or serfs, mainly conquered non-Aryan peoples; and below all these the terribly poor and oppressed outcastes. Among all the complexities of this system, to this day the Brahmans however poor remain the religious aristocrats of Hinduism, wearing the sacred cord, hedged about with custom and tradition more complex and inescapable than those of the Pharisee of the New Testament era.

The story starts in 1857, when the suppression of the Mutiny led to the annexation of India under the British Crown. It ends in 1919, before the years of struggle which led to the independence and partition of India and Pakistan in 1947. Lakshmi Gokhale and Narayan Tilak were Brahmans, born and nurtured in strict households where the laws of religious observance and purification were meticulously honoured, and to lose caste was the greatest of all disasters. But in 1895, at the age of thirty-four, Tilak was baptized into the Christian faith. After five years of separation, passed in tears and prayers, his wife rejoined him with their son Dattu; and later she too became a Christian.

Tilak died in 1919. Lakshmibai survived him by many years, and in the nineteen-thirties published her reminiscences, *Smriti Chitre*. These were translated by Josephine Inkster and published by the Oxford University Press under the title *I Follow After*. Lakshmibai's was the more remarkable an achievement, because she herself was without any schooling as a child, and learnt to read and write under the impatient tuition of her own husband. She too wrote verse, at first in self-defence against a poetic husband who would write poems about their domestic crises; but later she learnt the art of composing and singing *kirtans*, stories chanted to the accompaniment of Indian musical instruments, and in this way she became an evangelist of the Gospel. After her husband's death she set herself to the task of completing the epic Life of Christ, *Christayan*, which he had planned and begun but characteristically forsaken time and time again as other interests crowded his eager mind and diverted his talents and attention.

CHAPTER ONE

THE HOLY MAN AND HIS CHILDREN

Some of these few first memories are but tales overheard.

My mother and my aunt were standing in the temple at Trimbak when Mother said to her, "My next child, no matter whether it is a boy or a girl, I shall give to you." My aunt had no children, and this was all that Mother could do to comfort her. She kept her promise and, as I was her next baby, I grew up under my aunt's roof. It might even be said that my brothers and sisters too were brought up by her. We had no great love for our own home. We children, our mother, and grandmother had all to endure such persecution that we were only too glad to escape to our aunt. Father had become "holy", a word which you will understand better as you read this story, and in his "holiness" all our troubles had their roots. The cause was as follows.

1857. The days of Mutiny! Mother's father was a keeper of the treasury of the god in the Hindu temple at Trimbak. He also acted as village banker for the local people and hill-tribes of the district. He was trusted by all the poor, and generally beloved by the village. This however did not prevent his prosperity giving rise to jealousy, and his enemies, taking advantage of the confusion during the rebellion, poisoned the minds of the Government officials against him. Grandfather was arrested in Trimbak and hanged on the spot.

Father was in Nasik when he heard this news. He

loved Grandfather as dearly as if he had been his own father, and as soon as he heard the manner of his death, he rose and went out into a lonely place in the jungle of Tapowan.

It was morning when he left the house. He did not return till the lamps were being lit. He had already bathed and washed his clothes; they were still wet on his body, it being the Hindu custom for religious ceremonies to put on freshly washed clothes before they can be contaminated by contact with any thing considered unclean.

"Where have you been?" everyone asked.

"I went to Tapowan. A low-caste Mahar was rinsing his mouth; a drop of his water splashed on to me, and I am defiled. Pour water over me, but do not touch me. I must bathe again."

From that day till his death, twenty-five years later, Father clung tenaciously to his rites of purification. These brought not only his own house but the whole village to the verge of despair. He held himself contaminated even by the touch of another Brahman, a man of his own caste. When the women of the house went out to a *haldi-kunku* ceremony, on their return he insisted that they should bathe and even wash their hair before coming in.

The news of Grandfather's execution had been too great a shock for his mind. From henceforth all things in contact with the outside world were considered unclean until they had been specially washed.

Some twelve years after Father had become "holy" I was born (1870).

In front of the entrance gate of our house was a low earthen platform, immediately inside was the cow-shed, in the centre an open courtyard, and beyond that a veranda. The household shrine was at the left of the

15

veranda, and behind it lay the kitchen. The shrine had a great big window like a door. To anyone sitting there every last stick and stone was visible. That was where Father always sat.

He used to go out every morning at eight o'clock, and return in the evening at six. As we had no watches in those days, the sun falling on the coping meant eight o'clock, and the cattle coming home in the evening meant six o'clock. As soon as he came in, he bathed, then said his prayers, fingered his rosary and made his offering to the gods. His stern eye watched even the kitchen. Among Hindus, cooking is considered almost a religious rite, so whoever was doing it—and this was invariably my mother—had first to bathe and wash her *sari*, and put it on again still wet. Everything had to be done with the right hand, the left (which is "unclean") hanging on one side as if broken. It took at least two hours for Father to finish his evening prayers and all his acts of worship. By that time dinner would be ready, and at ten or eleven at night he would dine.

We were a family of five brothers and sisters. There had been several others, but only five of us survived. My oldest sister was Bhiku; after her came my brothers, Keshav, Bhagirathi, and Vishnu, and lastly myself. Not one of us ever sat near Father, or dined with him. Even on high days and holidays it was the same. This by no means implies that he paid no attention to his children. From the window of the shrine his severe eyes followed everyone and everything.

All our neighbours were high-caste Brahmans like ourselves, yet even if one of them came to call, Mother had to sprinkle water over their footprints when they left, to purify the ground made "unclean" by their touch. Nevertheless, when Father was out of the house in the morning, there was no lack of fun for all. As soon

16

as his back was turned the women nearby gathered in our house, and we children collected our friends to play. Mother always hungered for companionship. She would bathe other people's babies, comfort the young daughter-in-law, dispense medicine to one, speak kindly to another. She even went into a Maratha woman's house once, and baked big flat cakes with brown sugar stuffing, though the Marathas are of a lower caste than ours and no Brahman can touch them. But all this she did secretly. Father's rule was another story. To him everything brought in from outside was "unclean" and had to be washed, down to the very salt and pepper. Once he ordered his children to wash the salt. They determined to reform him, and tying up the salt in a piece of cloth they soaked it well and hung it on a peg. In no time the salt had dissolved, and drained out. When Father came to look into the bag, behold, there was nothing. From that day on, salt, sugar, oil and clarified butter were permitted to go unwashed.

The washing of all things fell for the most part to Mother and Grannie. According to orders they washed everything, or at least made a pretence of washing; and so long as they did it themselves the salt and sugar never dissolved. Many and many a time they practised deception, and taught us to dissemble too, but not without reason—for when the grain was brought in from the fields, Father demanded that it should be washed before it was stored. How could they wash twenty bushels of corn at a time? They washed a little of it, and spread that over the rest of the heap. When Father came home in the evening, he would question all the children. They had been well coached beforehand, and for the most part told the same story; but if one took fright and told the truth inadvertently, then the whole household would be thrown into confusion. At that late hour of night everything that had been polluted must be washed under Father's eye, the children must be well whipped for telling lies, and lastly Father himself, being contaminated by them, must bathe again. We endured this inquisition every evening.

Having answered the call of nature in the morning, Father needed four lumps of earth, each as big as a coconut, with which to rub his hands and feet clean. For twenty-five years, without a break, he brought this earth from the jungle two or three miles away, from a certain place where no one was ever likely to go and contaminate it. They say a great pit is to be found there even now. Taking this earth he would sit hour after hour "purifying" his hands and feet.

In those days Hindu children were married to each other at the age of five or six, or younger, and to have a girl of eleven years unmarried was an unheard-of thing. I was nearly eleven, well fed and cared for, and with no troubles. I looked older than my years. My Aunt and Uncle Govindrao were nearly out of their minds with anxiety about my marriage, but he was not prepared to look for a husband for me. He used to say to my parents, "You make the choice, I won't. I cannot risk anyone saying that I married the child to the first boy that turned up, just to save the expense of keeping her." He was quite prepared to bear the expense of my wedding.

But Father, fully occupied with his purifications, had no time to choose my husband; even if he had had time, he would never have found a son-in-law "holy" enough to please him. Mother too was worried, but she was only a woman; what could she do?

About this time a student called Narayan Vaman Tilak was becoming famous in Nasik as a poet and eloquent speaker. Pendse, my brother-in-law, urged Uncle Govindrao to write to Wamanrao Tilak, the boy's father, inviting him to come and see me.

Wamanrao replied, "I will not sell my son for a dowry. If you will pay what you can for the wedding I shall do likewise. The only thing I insist on is that the girl's horoscope must be auspicious, otherwise I cannot give my consent to the match. Also, there are no women in my house. You must look after the girl until she is old enough to live with her husband. I do not need to see her. I shall be pleased if everyone on the spot is pleased."

We were all greatly delighted with this letter. My horoscope, astrological calculations, and records had been prepared beforehand. Uncle Govindrao desired nothing better than to let me stay with him until I grew up. Only one thing remained, to send me to Nasik for the approval of the bridegroom.

Tilak's friends came with him for the interview, and agreed that I would do. I marvel that Tilak should have been pleased with me, for in appearance and colour I was very ordinary. For the rest, though my eyes and nose were not beautiful, they were at least there, and in the right place.

I had only to face my grandmother-in-law now, and in this examination too I passed. Gangabai, pinching the lobe of my left ear sharply, announced, "I approve of the girl." When my ear was pinched, I neither exclaimed nor drew in my breath, so she must have decided that I could be taken anywhere by anyone who liked to lead me by the ear.

Uncle Govindrao had made up his mind to spend no less than a thousand rupees on the wedding. It was quite evident what my father would do! My mother would have done anything and everything, but it was not in her hands, poor thing. Her only comfort, in the kind of life she led at home, was to dispense kindness to others as far as possible, and to toil for others as long as she had strength. God must have created people like my Aunt and Uncle Govindrao to help to look after her children, as a reward for her virtue. Mother could neither read nor write, but as a recreation she used to compose songs and teach them to the neighbours' daughters and young brides. This was the comforting oil she used on the labouring wheels of household care. Now, what could she do more than look at my uncle with eyes filled with tears of gratitude?

Uncle Govindrao regarded this wedding as if it had been that of a child of his own. Indeed, he did more for me than he would have done for his own daughter. He wrote to Wamanrao Tilak saying, "I have a good standing in the village and the wedding must be in keeping. Jalalpur is quite a small place, and I should like you to give a dinner to the whole village." Waman rao agreed.

He arrived four days before the wedding, bringing with him no less than twelve bullock-carts laden with guests. Our house was bursting with them, and a pavilion was erected in front of our door. Only then did he meet his daughter-in-law.

So far all had gone well. Now appeared a Himalayan obstacle. The lineage of the Gokhales and Tilaks is from Kashyap and Shandilya respectively, and those two lines cannot mix! How could there be any marriage?

Uncle Govindrao then decided to have me formally adopted into his family. I, who was a Gokhale, should become a Khambete by Hindu law. Peace reigned. But at the time of the adoption ceremony Father could not be found! Following his inflexible rule, he had gone off into the jungle to fetch his ball of earth. There was no hope of his returning before nightfall. Would that man give a thought to his daughter's adoption ceremony, who could send a message to his mother on her death-bed, "Wait! Do not die till I finish my evening prayers"?

Uncle Govindrao was furious. He was never known to lose his temper, but this time he was properly indignant. My aunt was in a passion too, and her wrath poured from her lips in a steady stream. My mother was as one dead. It seemed as if the marriage would be broken off for a mere trifle. The spirits of the wedding party were completely damped. There was dismay and confusion everywhere.

Then, in the nick of time, one of our relations came to Mother's rescue. He produced a text from the Hindu Scriptures proving that a mother has authority to give away her daughter. The text was like a few drops of cold water to milk about to boil over. Peace reigned again. Her eyes wet with tears, Mother gave me to Uncle Govindrao.

In two or three days the wedding ceremony was completed. Uncle Govindrao gave me away.

The next day was the Hindu fast *Ekadashi*, when only a certain type of food may be eaten. All the bridegroom's relations rose up in a body to demand its due observance. There were a dozen cart-loads of guests from a dozen different houses. There was no saying what each would want. Plenty of light dishes had been prepared, but they were all set aside, and every man served with his heart's desire. The bride-groom's friends stole from the bride's, and when they were found out, laughed and said it was all a joke. There was plenty of fun at our wedding!

On those occasions the bridegroom is encouraged to have a fit of the sulks; so too at our wedding. Tilak was carefully instructed what to do. He had never sulked in his life. He would fly into a temper, but of sulking he knew nothing. Nevertheless his friends said to him, "When you are called for dinner, do not get up and go. Say you want a ring, two *tolas* in weight, and sit tight." So at one o'clock, when my brother went to call him for dinner, Tilak answered, "I am sulking, I shall come when my people come." The people on our side of the house were hungry; they had already eaten a little on the sly before sitting down to wait for the bridegroom. But the bridegroom was hungry too. Quietly he called my brother aside and whispered, "Brother, I am hungry." Full of joy Keshav began to serve the dinner, and a message was sent to my father-in-law and his party, "Dinner is served, Tilak has sat down to dine, and the rice is getting cold." Enough! They all came running to sit down too, and no one so much as mentioned the ring.

Tilak liked none of the usual games, such as the bride and bridegroom trying their strength over a *supari* nut hidden in the hand, exchanging glasses of water, or feeding each other; but in spite of him they all had to be carried through. There was none of the usual quarrelling and ill-feeling from beginning to end.

A dinner for the whole village had been prepared, and afterwards the bridal party returned to Nasik. That night saw the bridal procession, and the state entrance of the bride into her new home.

My husband was eighteen years old, and I was eleven.

CHAPTER TWO

NON-MONOTONOUS MARRIED LIFE

I never saw my mother-in-law, for she died before my marriage. She was in disfavour with Wamanrao her husband because of her love for Tilak and his love for her. Tilak and his brother Mahadev were their father's black sheep; he was suspicious of them because the lines on their hands did not conform to his ideas. His estimation of a person depended on goblins, sorcery, demon-possession, luck, planets, horoscopes, and the length and shape of fingers and toes.

As a boy Tilak was very badly treated by his father, and once ran away to Poona and was not heard of again for six months. Only when Wamanrao was transferred to another place, and left his family behind, were they at peace. From the very first Tilak worshipped his mother. It is no exaggeration to say that from her hands he quaffed his first dose of poetry. She used to compose poems, which were destroyed in the flames of the stove and the devouring furnace of Wamanrao's wrath. Wamanrao in anger was like a tiger gnashing his teeth. It was as a result of a brutal assault on his own wife, in the presence of Tilak, that she died, leaving her children to the care of the world, with the name of God, *Ram, Ram*, on her lips.

Tilak was only eleven or twelve years old then. Wamanrao was scorched with remorse when he saw what his own thoughtlessness had brought upon him, and ceased to torment his son. Together they went to scatter her ashes on the waters of the river Godaveri, according to the Hindu custom; and Tilak ran away to Nasik, where he found refuge and a welcome in a poor Brahman's house. As Tilak made friends in the town, he earned a few rupees a month bringing vegetables from the market for other households.

He had a great desire to learn Sanskrit, and began his studies in the Vedic scriptures or *Shastras*. His remarkable intelligence was recognized, and he was greatly beloved by all his teachers. So he began to forget both his father's severity and his mother's love. He never forgot the goddess of Poetry, Nature and Oratory.

He was living in Nasik when first we met, and our first home was there, in 1880.

How many homes there were to be in the next fifteen years! Soon we had to leave Nasik, and went back to Jalalpur. Uncle Govindrao was as fond of Tilak as if he were his father. My aunt saw things from a different angle: if the son-in-law were spoilt by keeping him idle at home, what would happen later? There were everlasting squabbles between them over this. My aunt would say, "Tilak has no sense of responsibility at all. If he has been fed twice in the day, then off he goes with some worthless fellow." To this Uncle Govindrao would answer, "Let him alone. When he is young he will behave like that. Later his sense of responsibility will develop."

Tilak found plenty of friends and an appreciative audience for his poetry. He began to take part in plays, but as stealthily as a thief, to keep the least whisper from my uncle's ears. Yet in spite of all this care the secret leaked out. My uncle used to lock our door from the outside after we had gone to bed, and tried to put a padlock on the mouths of men who praised Tilak's acting to him. At last he went to hear for himself, and when Tilak began to sing his own songs, the rising tears in Uncle Govindrao's eyes put out the fires of anger. His wrath was damped; but the thunderstorm my aunt was piling up broke with a crash. At last what was to come came. Tilak heard what my aunt had said. "He doesn't look after his household affairs: this son-in-law is more than we bargained for." We decided to go back to Nasik.

It never took Tilak long to translate an idea into action. Back he went, and started a private English school. He carried out this responsible work with the utmost devotion, and his whole time was spent with the children.

But now Wamanrao summoned us to Poona, and Tilak obeyed his father's orders. One of his chief characteristics was that he became absorbed in whatever was before his eyes for the moment. Once a thing was out of sight, many a time he would not so much as remember its existence. What then could be left of care and concern? His own poem, *O bird, wilt thou return?* might well be quoted against him. Many and many a time when he went out it was our turn to say, "Wilt thou fly away and be diffused, like a breath of the wind?" Whenever Tilak disappeared, I would sit and cry, the old people in the house would be filled with anxiety, and the young men would form a search party.

In Poona, after a time, Tilak took my only gold-bordered *sari*, pawned it, and disappeared. Father and son must have fallen out about something. I found myself alone in my father-in-law's clutches. I was only thirteen at the time. Meanwhile Tilak's impetuous rush carried him far away, and he became the disciple of a holy ascetic. He used to sit in the river repeating his vows over and over. Gathering the bitter leaves from the neem tree, he pounded them on a stone, rolled them into balls and ate them. Others began to gather round him, and he retired to the woods to meditate. But one day his teacher asked him with whom he lived at home, and whether he had left them with their permission. The only answer was "No", and he was ordered back to Jalalpur at once, whither I had returned to my uncle.

There he appeared; he had a rosary of sacred berries as big as limes round his neck, a long robe to cover him, his beard and matted hair had grown to an astonishing length. At the sight of this apparition Uncle Govindrao was greatly perturbed, but he made up his mind to say nothing, and warned my aunt not to speak. She held her tongue well in check, but a leopard cannot change his spots, and one day Tilak overheard her blaming my uncle for the marriage.

"To have chosen a crow that has hardly alighted on a perch before it is off again!" At this a thunderclap was heard outside! Tilak packed his belongings into a bundle, and we were off.

This time we went back to Wamanrao, and Tilak opened another school. As usual it was a great success; he loved his scholars as children, and they honoured him as their father. The syllabus was of his own devising, and his main desire was to create true gentlemen. Even if they learned nothing else, they could learn good manners from their association with him.

My father-in-law was an exceedingly tidy and methodical man. He never married again, but did his own cooking, and that so economically that after dinner not a grain of rice was left over. His family came from Konkan, south of Bombay, mine from the Deccan; and this ill-starred, illiterate Deccani daughter could not cook Konkani food for him.

"Lakshmi, this will not do. The people in your home may have been animals; I am not. From tomorrow the cooking must be properly done."

When I sat down to cook, he used to sit in the front room where he could see what was happening in the kitchen. Often at one and the same moment he would be worshipping his gods and teaching me to cook.

He was always furious if he was asked for anything. I had neither oil nor soap for my hair, but whenever I asked he would reply, "Grind, earn, and buy your own oil and soap." I used to wash my hair with earth. Sometimes when I sat down to bathe he would lift the hot water from under my nose and go and bathe himself; I had to finish in cold water. He had one reply to our usual wrangles:

"Once the wood was finished. My wife was pregnant; all the same I made her chop it. What irks you then? My wife never retorted. When anything in the house was nearly finished, she brought what was left and placed it before me in silence. Then I knew that it was finished. Girls nowadays are most forward. You will never learn how to behave before your elders."

Meanwhile Tilak's poems were becoming famous throughout Bombay and Poona. I had trouble enough in the house, but these were good days for him. He would go off to lecture, and enjoy himself too well; neither sign nor word would come from him, till I was most anxious. At last my father-in-law refused to keep me any longer, and Tilak took me to Bombay. I was utterly bewildered by the many-storied buildings, the trams and streets. From the moment I arrived at the station I was stupefied, and did not know where I was going. I was continually looking around me, and Tilak had to warn me to watch my step. I was so enchanted by the astonishing sights that just hearing street cries I kept running out to look.

In this way, popping my head out and staring down the street, whom should I see suddenly but Uncle Govindrao, walking along with his neck craned upwards and his mouth gaping. He had been searching for me for three days, to tell me that my father was dying. He took me back to Jalalpur, but my father had died.

In 1884, when I was fourteen, my first son was born. Tilak had left me at Jalalpur and disappeared for six months without any letter. Competitions in oratory were being held in many places, and Tilak had a passion for giving lectures; he nearly always won a prize, and squandered or gave away the prize money. He was just as happy without any money: I used to say to him, "No sooner have you money in your pocket than you are troubled how to get rid of it." I was the opposite, always anxious about how to keep it. To throw money away is easy, so in this battle of ours he always won. It was ever he who made the debts, and I who paid them.

Our son Vidayanand died, and God gave us a daughter, Mai. Tilak had no treasure in the world like her, but she too died. Then came another son, Dattu, who my aunt was convinced was Govindrao reborn; and yet another son, Mahadev, who died as a baby.

Tilak still appeared and disappeared, and had many professions. He was a printer in Bombay, he kept a fireworks shop (and let off all the fireworks), he was a tutor, a student of medicine, teacher and poet, editor and thinker. In 1893 we went to live for two years in Rajnandgaon, the most crucial years of Tilak's life. We were living in a small State under a Raja, and

28

Tilak tried very hard to put an end to the oppression of the labourers in the State. He was in some danger of being thrown into prison; and either on account of this agitation, or because he was likely to become a Christian, some people wished to get him into trouble. He kept all his papers under lock and key; and when he was out, people came to me and asked to see his correspondence and papers. But I would never let them do so.

As soon as he came to Rajnandgaon, Tilak undertook a big programme of reading and study. He employed a *munshi* to help him to master Urdu. He used to read many English books, and a few were committed to memory. It also appears from his diary that he was reading the Bible with avidity. He was also keeping up a correspondence with the famous Christian writer Baba Padmanji and with Dr. Abbott. Probably on their recommendation, he must have read the lives of great Indian Christians, and a comparison of the Hindu and Christian religions. That he should write to so many people, that so many should come and discuss with him, seemed to me rather strange, but I had no conception of the depth of his intrigues.

As for my own reading and writing, I was doing my best, but the results were not up to Tilak's expectations. Fathomless is my achievement in learning from beginning to end! Pencil, nib, the end of a pen, or even a match will do for me. Tilak says in his diary (7 February, 1894): "My gentleman Dattu is singing. I am teaching him this verse: 'God, give me the strength to play, to see the happiness of the world, to please my father and mother. Lord, hear my prayer.' Lakshmi is writing down the verse with the end of a match. Though I tell her a line a hundred times she cannot do it. What innumerable mistakes! She is the very spit and image of her aunt, a hard worker but with a shrewish tongue."

His enthusiasm for the Bible gave rise to sharp encounters with the neighbours, one of whom cursed the Bible: "This led to an argument between us. Lakshmi got angry and broke in like a fool. We had a small quarrel over it."

Nevertheless, the reading of the Bible, and in particular the Sermon on the Mount, began to have an effect on him. He was very repentant about that quarrel. Later on he himself says, "There is in me no forgiveness, no peace, nothing; alas, alas, all my learning and thought are but vanity."

About the Christian religion he writes on 18 February, 1894: "My mind is being drawn towards the religion of Christ. Here appears a faith capable of giving the mind of man peace, devotion, righteousness, salvation. Better to live in this small garden of Christianity, forever filled with flowers and fruits, than to inhabit the boundless spaces of Hinduism, with its thorns and trees, deep rivers, terrible mountains, fearful deserts and pleasing mango groves. Yet today I have not the courage to let such a sentence fall from my lips. Lakshmi gets tired even of reading. I am held back only by fear of her, and love of her. O God! Guide her and guide me."

In the end Tilak sent in his resignation, and I went back to Nasik. Tilak had left me on the journey, but he turned up after a week. Everyone was advising him what to do next; he replied that he should be a singer and go round giving *kirtans*. But for that he would need musical instruments, and must go to Bombay to get them.

A little later it was published in many papers that Tilak had become a Christian.

CHAPTER THREE

TILAK BECOMES A CHRISTIAN

This is what Tilak himself wrote about his conversion.

"You all know that any seeker after truth, who tries to assess the worth of the Holy Bible in the strength of his own deficient judgment, finds the miracles of Christ as related in the New Testament lying in his path like mountains. That Seeker will have an acquaintance with the Son of Man. He is not yet worthy to understand the Son of God. The Crucified he knows, but to comprehend the risen Lord is beyond him. The best way to bring conviction to such a Seeker is to pray with him. Through the great golden door of prayer he should repeatedly be brought into the presence of the Father, and in his heart should be awakened a true love of the merciful Father of this world. In this way he will come to know the Father, and his doubts about the miracles will be removed naturally. I have always thought that God Himself resolves such difficult questions for the true Seeker.

"Round a new convert—and such am I, because it is only eleven months since I was converted—rather than lovers of the truth gather those whose pride is in idol-worship, heretics who sit conning negations, or those who understand nothing, having no desire to understand, and no ability in them beyond that of making mischief: such a crowd as this will gather. Many of these people laughed at me for being so mad as to believe in miracles. For all these I have one reply. I say to them: 'See, I myself am a walking, speaking miracle. Look at me.'

"At least to those who know me, here is an irrefutable miracle. Am I not a Christian? Have I not full faith in my Lord Christ? Only two years ago was I not the sworn enemy of this Christ and His followers? With this hand, now so eager in His service, how many papers have I scribbled off in the heat of my scorn for Him? This tongue, which today is always ready to witness to the one great mercy of Christ, has heretofore poured what unrestrained contempt on that Holy Name?

"In former days did anyone think, or even dream, that I would become a Christian? Could anyone have conceived in those days that this man, so proud of the Hindu religion, would propose to forsake it, and glorying in the Bible, abandon himself to the Will of God?

"Nevertheless this my pride perished, and today I stand like a small child before God holding the hand of Christ. Is it any wonder that people should see this and be astonished? I myself am astonished at myself. What other miracle is needed? There is no question of the truth of this wonder.

"Truly, Brothers and Sisters, herein is a miracle, that this was the mercy of God. I had no intention of becoming a Christian, but that Good Shepherd leaving His ninety-nine lambs searched for me amongst the terrible mountains, and brought me in. What overflowing pride and arrogance were lodged in my breast! I who was going to found a new religion myself have become a disciple of Jesus. Blessed be the Lord! Truly all blessing be His!

"It is true I was trying to establish a new religion for India, and not only that, but I also wished to

32

evolve one by which all the nations of the world, being bound in one brotherhood, would be united in spirit. I was engrossed in this thought for many years. Later by the merciful hand of God this idea was set a foundation stone in my heart for the building of the great temple of Christianity.

"No work is accomplished at once. I became a Christian. To describe exactly the succession of reasons behind this event will not take long. It is enough that my mother was a very religious and loving woman. How she attained to such a virtue I do not know. I never remember her to have mentioned the name of Christ, but *Live in the fear of God, Be kind to everyone*, were the sermons she always preached to us. I have never seen another woman who performed as she did her holy, maternal duties.

"There is no need to let any question arise as to how a worshipper of idols could be so, because we know that God for His own particular purpose can endow an idol-worshipper with virtue and make her His instrument.

"Also, when I was young I had a teacher whose heart was flooded with love of his country, though he never understood how best to serve it. He filled our small heads with a madness of love to match his own.

"I remember well when I was still small sitting in my class with a geography lesson in progress; but only my body was there, my mind was travelling far away, lost in deep thoughts of what would happen to India in the future. Even in childhood I was stirred to anger when I saw the caste distinctions of my country. I was only fourteen or fifteen when in a boys' meeting I spoke on this subject. Have the Brahmans a monopoly over alms and charity? I remember my father remarking, half in fun and half in anger, 'This boy will be outcasted some day.'

"I never remember being under a teacher who was bound down by ancient customs. For the most part I fell in with teachers with progressive ideas. As a result I formed the habit of regarding all subjects with an open mind. These teachers gave me courage of thought, speech and manner. In the whole of my childhood it was never my fate to meet with such intimidation as would interfere with my freedom of thought. It was my firm conviction that, if India was to return to prosperity, it would be by the great door of religion. Therefore according to my ability I gave myself up to the study of Religion and Philosophy.

"Finally at Nagpur I found a true patron, Appasaheb. To this day I honour that worthy man as my father. He had accumulated much knowledge about Hindu Vedas and the Science of the Supreme Spirit manifested in the Individual Self. For three years I dwelt in that ocean of meditation and spiritual knowledge. At last I prepared the philosophical foundations for my new religion:

1. The Creator of the world is some particular, personal Spirit, and He regards all mankind as His children.
2. All scriptures are the work of men, and there is only one book giving a knowledge of God—that book is the world.
3. There is no such thing as former birth or reincarnations. The sorrows and joys of man are dependent on a man's heredity, his own spirit and his attitude towards his duty in society.
4. Faith in God and brotherhood of men on this earth is the essence of all religion.
5. There is no sin equal to idol-worship.

34

"In pursuit of the foundation of these ideas I must have become as abstracted as one of the ancient sages. I began to study the lives of the founders of different religions. With many of them I did not agree. However, in Gautama Buddha I found one to my liking, and I thought of copying him except for his mistakes. The astonishing thing is that not even into my dreams did the Bible or Christ enter, the chief reason being the extremely simple language of the Bible. It has become the very birthmark of a Brahman that he will only turn his mind to incomprehensible subjects or those which will exercise his utmost intelligence.

"If the Sanskrit books in the Hindu religion were translated into everyday speech, and put into the hands of the Brahmans, I am convinced they would regard them as rubbish and throw them away. If someone begins to repeat an incantation of which not even one letter is understood, then are the people pleased. These same words translated would only be ridiculed. This is one reason for not looking to the Christian religion.

"But there is another far greater. I never met a Christian preacher, nor did any religious book in Marathi fall into my hands, that could arouse my interest. I had not even read one or two pages of the Bible. I had only heard and read plenty of things against it.

"I saw the Christians of my own country, but the unspiritual state of those I saw was deplorable. I used to think the only difference between Christians and idol-worshippers was in their eating and drinking and customs. These then were the causes that separated me from Christ and the Christian religion.

"In the year 1893, to please my patron, I agreed to start a new magazine on Religion and Philosophy.

35

Two issues were published, and then because of my new beliefs I had to give up the editor's chair.

"The Raja of the small state of Rajnandgaon offered me work, and I boarded the train. There is another class between second and third, called Intermediate, by which I meant to travel. But when I came to the carriage, a European was sitting there. I expected the usual experience of being turned out. Nothing of the sort happened; on the contrary, smiling a little, he made room for me.

"Here, O reader, I will suggest one thing to you. Many European travellers and servants by their behaviour in trains become positive mountains in the way of the spread of Christianity. The Hindu people have a laughable ignorance about the religion, but all the same they have some conception of how a man called Christian should behave. Add to that the belief that every white man is a Christian, and Christianity is stained in their eyes by the evil behaviour of one Sahib. The trains and stations are filled with people who, by their bullying manner, deal deadly blows to the Kingdom of Christ. May God send a servant to teach people on the railways what love is. Enough!

"My companion in the compartment was extremely polite and gentle, so that anyone would have been drawn towards him. I had with me only one book to read, a well-beloved book of Sanskrit poems; and we talked for a long time on poetry and poets. He knew a little Sanskrit, and was familiar with its literature.

"Slowly he turned the conversation, and questioned me about my opinion of the Christian religion. I told him my idea of a new religion. When he heard of it, he said with the greatest gravity, 'I think that, counting from today, within two years you will be a Christian.' I was astounded at this; I felt his prophecy was nothing short of lunacy. But we continued talking for a long time, and he said, 'Young man, God is drawing you. Study the Bible. Apply yourself whole-heartedly to the life of Christ, and in truth you will become a Christian.'

"Considering this an exceedingly rash speech, I cursed it in my heart. Lastly he prayed, took out a New Testament, and gave it to me. I disliked the book at sight; however, I promised to read it. I did not promise, thinking there would be any meaning in the book, but only for the sake of gratifying this good man. We said an affectionate farewell. It is a strange thing that to the end neither of us asked the other's name or dwelling-place.

"At Rajnandgaon I was teacher, Clerk of the Royal Court, and Government Clerk. Towards the end I also took up the work of Sheriff. However, for a man with a passion for reading, there was little there to occupy the mind, and all my most beloved Sanskrit books were in Nagpur. This forced me to keep my promise. I decided to follow my usual practice of reading the book through from beginning to end, marking the passages worthy of more thought. But I only got as far as the Sermon on the Mount.

"It became impossible to leave these jewel-like sentences, so filled with love, mercy and truth. The most difficult questions of Hindu philosophy found their answer in these three chapters of Saint Matthew. I was most astonished to see problems like that of re-birth fully resolved, and filled with desire for more knowledge of Christ I read eagerly on to the end. A Christian Police Superintendent gave me a little book and bundles of tracts. Among them I found a book called *The Character of Jesus*. After reading it my hunger for a knowledge of the life of Christ grew.

"Christ has said, 'Ask, and thou shalt receive.' One

day, doubting this promise, I thought like any foolish immature boy that I would put it to the test. I made my petition: 'May I receive here and quickly a history of Palestine and an account of the life and period of Christ.' To this prayer I added, 'If I do not receive the fruit for my asking, then for evermore I shall hold it false that God hears and answers prayer.' This was mere folly, but God had mercy on His poor child. The very next day I was suddenly transferred from one office to another. When I got there, what should I see but, under the rubbish in a box, three beautiful books; two of them were very big, nearly as big as Webster's big dictionary, and one was called *Beautiful Stories and Jewels of Virtuous Thoughts*. In these three books I found the information I wanted. Now one after another God sent answers to my prayers. I was dumb with astonishment. My mind became riveted on Christ.

"After some months I began to feel that in spirit I was a Christian, but love of my people and love of honour led me into temptation, and I ignominiously denied it.

"It is difficult for others to understand the persecution that must be endured, when his caste-brothers find out that some high-caste Hindu has become a Christian. Though God may have been far from me at other times, in time of trouble He was near me, as a mother is near her child night and day when it is ill and crying. From all kinds of trouble He saved me. How many times and with how many men have I played hide-and-seek in most ignoble fear, but God did not abandon such a sinner. I lost my work, I was reduced to an extremity of poverty; I had to go away leaving my only child. My wife with whom up till today I have lived as object and shadow, after great indecision at last clings to her own people; but God has not deserted me. In the end of November, 1894, three nights running someone came and said to me in my sleep: 'Follow Him. Do not be afraid.' Then could I restrain myself no more; though there were so many difficulties in the way of my baptism, I was resolved to make it known at once to the world that I was a Christian, and thereupon requested Dr. J. E. Abbott of the American Board of Foreign Missions to publish this fact. He announced it in the *Dnyanodaya*, Indian Christian magazine, and my greatest desire was fulfilled. May God be praised, I was baptized on 10 February, 1895, in Bombay in the American Mission Church. The prophecy made two years earlier in the train by that stranger had come true. God had drawn me to Himself, and even today with overwhelming loving-kindness He guides forward His weak child."

Tilak sought out the American Mission High School in Bombay and met Dr. Justin Abbott, with whom he had been corresponding for a long time. After they had made him study the Christian religion for four months, he was baptized.

It is possible to say that the course of the thought of the Christian community was changed from the day of Tilak's baptism. From that time Dr. Abbott became his *guru* or preceptor in religion, although he was baptized by the Reverend Tukaramji Nathoji, because he expressed the determination not to be baptized by any foreigner but by the hand of an Indian.

The news of his baptism spread like wildfire on all sides. It was heard at once in Nasik. All his friends and relatives began to come in a steady stream to see my brother-in-law Pendse, but in the house they sat in silence and no one said a word about it. Some of them would turn towards me and Dattu, screw up their faces and wipe their eyes. When I saw this pantomime,

I fell into an indescribable state of mind. I wondered if Tilak had been killed in some terrible accident. "A man's own mind is his worst enemy."

Pendse sat stolidly leaning his head outside the window, his brow clasped tightly in his hands. We gazed at one another with vacant eyes. No one spoke. At the most we just wiped away our tears.

Dattu was in an extraordinary position. People were forever lifting him up, or giving him something to eat, but no one would speak. When I saw all this, the strength in my hands and knees turned to water.

My brother Keshav went to Bombay and searched every mission until he found Tilak, who told him, "I have become a Christian. Look after your sister; see that she does not commit suicide."

"Whether she lives or dies, you have now nothing to do with her," answered Keshav. As he left, he saw that the sacred lock of hair on Tilak's head had been cut, and he sobbed aloud. However angry he had tried to appear, his eyes had been brimming over from the beginning; now the very last tear was drained out of his heart.

As soon as Keshav returned home, he went to the bed where my sister Bhiku lay, and told her everything. She was nearly choked with tears.

"Tell Lakshmi anything you like," she said. "I cannot say a word to her." I was called upstairs. I was so overcome with apprehension that I could not climb the steps. Like a small child, drawing myself up by my hands I came, and sat before my brother and sister. My brother began a sermon: how many chaste and dutiful wives had there been, Sita, Savitri, Tara and Draupadi, whose fame would last for ever. I broke in.

"I know all the scriptures. Did you call me to give

me a sermon? You went to Bombay to get word of Tilak. Tell me first, is he alive?"

"Yes, he is alive, safe, happy. He has got work as a teacher there, but . . . but. . . ."

"Then why 'But'?"

"He is a Christian."

"Then let him be one! Enough that he is somewhere, and that he is well. Though he has gone, he has not taken so much as a bit of skin off my forehead, or touched my fate written on it."

I rose and descended the stairs in a hurry. But at the bottom, the strength flowed out of me completely. The rest of the women in the house were waiting anxiously for me by the door. They had all heard the news before I had, and now began to comfort me. But all their words were as water poured on to an upturned vessel. I had become as stone, I could not shed a tear, my throat was dry.

In this family crisis, most of our relations came to spend the night with Pendse. No one ate any dinner. No one spoke a word. One after another they spread on the floor whatever they could find and lay down to sleep where they fell.

I was in the middle; on one side lay Keshav and on the other Bhiku; each of them had thrown an arm over me. At one or two o'clock sleep began to weave her net; every one was caught in it except me. Very gently I drew off the arms encircling me. Binding up the loose end of my sari tightly I looked for Dattu, but could not see him. Going to the front door I began to lift the wooden bar.

At that instant the night-watchman's "All's well" fell on my ears, making a new thought master of my mind. If these men should catch me and take me to the police station, and if there were an enquiry

41

on the morrow, the world would babble that I was the sister-in-law of such-and-such a man, and Pendse would be put to shame. It had been my intention to throw myself into a deep pool in the river, but I changed my mind and went and stood by the household well. Now came the thought that, if I committed suicide here, my body could not be retrieved without infinite trouble; and Pendse would have to hang his head for me. My ears were buzzing. I could see no way open before me.

I went back to bed and lay down. In a little while I grasped Keshav's hand so fiercely that he woke in a fright; then everyone woke and began asking each other, "What has happened?" Keshav managed to unclasp my hand, and with that it seemed that all the strength drained out of me. I was quite conscious, and knew all that was going on about me, but in no wise could I move.

Each one had a different remedy of his own to suggest. My jaws were locked. Some said I had had a shock, others that I had taken poison. Bhiju replied, "She has not a farthing; how could she buy poison?" Someone suggested I had swallowed powdered glass. A new kind of glass bangle had just appeared on the market, and my sister had bought nine of them for me; she at once counted them.

A doctor was brought. He could not find my pulse, and he also gave his opinion that I had taken poison. They tried to open my teeth and to pour a little medicine between them. I lay like a log of wood. My tongue was drawn together and covered with prickles which did not go away for a whole month. It was many days before my strength returned a little, and the flood-gates of my tears opened.

Many and many a time in the next five years

42

I was on the point of taking my life, but I believe it was never possible. It was characteristic of me to grope on through the darkness of despair, but still to keep to the road. It was not in me to lie down and die half-way, but rather to rebound like a rubber ball.

CHAPTER FOUR

LAKSHMIBAI'S DISCOVERIES

After three years, Pendse was transferred to Nagar, where Tilak was now working, and there was a large Christian community. So I was sent to my brothers at Jalalpur. There I was not allowed so much as to wash my own sari or care for Dattu, and I began to spend my time in worship of the gods, reading the Hindu scriptures, making offerings, telling my rosary, and continually repeating the name of God. I ate only once a day, and kept many a fast besides. All this was done as a propitiation to the gods in order that Tilak should come back into caste.

There is a big temple of Maruti, the monkey-god, at Jalalpur. I used to put a stick into his hand in the hope that he would chase after Tilak and bring him back. The people of the village had no idea who did this. Sometimes I would place a stone on his head: for I had heard the saying, "Who has laid a stone on your head?" meaning, "Who has compelled you to do such-and-such a thing?" I thought I might compel Maruti in my service. I began to write the name of Ram on slips of paper and stick them on Maruti's image from his head right down towards his feet; I believed that, before he would allow the holy name of Ram to be defiled by touching his feet, Maruti (who was a devoted slave of Ram) would prevent such a catastrophe by delivering me from my troubles.

This nearly cost me my life, for the village thought

a witch was practising her craft, and lay in wait for the sorcerer with sticks. But when they caught me they only said, "Go on with your remedies, and may you succeed in bringing Tilak back."

From the river back to the house I used to draw footsteps with white powder, so that Maruti might find the way to our house when he brought Tilak back. I made a vow to offer to the goddess a red flower every day; if I could not obtain a red flower, I fasted that day. To save me from this, my sisters-in-law would bring red flowers from anywhere; they never complained. All they said was, "She does no harm, causes no loss to others; why should we hurt her?"

To Jalalpur too came Tilak's daily letters, sometimes furious, sometimes in excess of fury an empty sheet of paper. I would only cry the more. Three times he came to see me, and the third time he brought a European woman with him, Miss Harvey the famous Zenana missionary of Nasik, always known as *Ayee* or mother. She wanted to mediate between us, but I blazed up at her. Thirty years later, when we came to Nasik, we had experience of her loving-kindness; and as she lay dying it was my name she called, "Lakshmibai, Lakshmibai."

While we were in Jalalpur, my two brothers' sons were six years old, Dattu was five, and everyone in the house began to think of investing them with the sacred thread of the Brahmans. It was decided to hold a ceremony for the three boys together. Some people, however, said that Dattu should not be included; if his father decided to take him away later, the money spent on the ceremony would be wasted.

But Keshav said, "Never mind. It will cost nothing to remove the thread from his shoulder. I shall have his investiture first, and then that of our boys." He had been to Nasik to ask an astrologer if the ceremony of all three could be performed that year, and the arrangement had been proclaimed auspicious.

Keshav had to make many journeys into Nasik to arrange for the ceremony. He brought further news one time, that a new disease had been discovered. While you were looking at him, one or two lumps would rise on a man's body, especially in his armpits and he would fall down dead. Great was the alarm caused in the village by this news. This was the first appearance of bubonic plague in Western India. I was to know much more about it in years to come.

The arrangements for the investiture were complete at last. I never went against my sisters-in-law, and they for their part would not endure to hear anyone say a word against me. Now they said to my brother, "If you like, limit what you do for our own sons, but Dattu's ceremony must be properly held. Do not do anything that might hurt Lakshmi. It is her one and only ceremony."

Keshav replied, "I am spending most on his investiture. Do not worry." However, an investiture cannot be held in a maternal uncle's house, nor on a maternal uncle's knee. What should be done? Keshav wrote a letter to Sakharam, Tilak's brother, inviting him to take part in the ceremony, but his reply was evasive. Then Keshav wrote to Pendse, my sister's husband; he too refused: "I have vowed no vow that Tilak should abandon his wife and that I should hold his son on my knee for his thread ceremony. I shall share as much of the expense as you like, but I cannot bear to be present."

Announcements had been sent out that Dattu's ceremony would be performed first and that of my brothers' sons later; only on the card sent to Tilak were the dates reversed. This was in order that he should not know the date of Dattu's investiture, but only that it had been arranged; it was feared that he might do something to obstruct the ceremony on the day, if he knew when it was to be. People wept for three days at Dattu's investiture. The village priest held him on his knee; he too was in tears, poor man, because he had no son. "This," said he, "is the state of a boy with a father, and this the state of men with no children." In short, Dattu's ceremony was well watered with the heart's tears of all the guests. With much weeping, but no other obstruction, Dattu received his sacred thread.

Just as the images of the gods were set out for the boys' ceremony, four enormous letters arrived from Tilak. They contained a tapestry of all that was in his mind. What was lacking? Everything was laid out even to a million curses and threats of the law. "Our brother-in-law has sent us the prescribed offering of robes for the ceremony," Keshav remarked.

Dattu's health was not good in Jalalpur; he had malaria, and two or three times a day would have shivering fits. He, for whose well-being I must spend my life, needed a change of air. Tilak's brother Sakharam was at Pandharpur, and Tilak secretly sent me the money for the journey.

But Keshav was against my going. "I do not approve of your going uninvited to someone who did not help in Dattu's thread ceremony by one farthing. If you go in spite of me, then never show me your face again." To which I replied, "It is not that I am pleased to go, but I must for Dattu's sake." My sister-in-law said, "If it is for Dattu's sake then go, but you are no trouble to us here. Only do not go to Tilak."

At Pandhapur Sakharam and his wife were waiting for us. According to the Indian custom they both greeted me, and said their house was mine; I was to treat them as I treated Dattu. They gave me the honour due to the wife of an elder brother; the running of the house was put into my hands. Here too I continued my religious exercises with great fervour and strictness.

Meanwhile Tilak and I were indulging in a furious correspondence. Sometimes his letters were most perverse, and I would go to the temple and sit for hours crying. I had time to do that, because I ate only once in the day. Sometimes people would reproach me, and I would be deeply hurt. Sometimes their arrows pierced right through my heart. On top of that, now and again, Sakharam would add to it, so that I was nearly out of my mind.

At the very time when I could endure no more, Tilak arrived. I was overjoyed, but Sakharam retired into silence and would speak to no one, not even his wife; even with his own year-old baby he was, as it were, not on speaking terms. Because he would not speak, the whole household undertook a vow of silence. As time went on, everyone became heartily tired of the situation. Tilak in the end broke the spell by saying, "I must arrange for Dattu's education. Now is the time for him to learn; once his education lags behind it is a lifelong loss. Come with me to Nagar. I shall rent a separate house for you."

"Why to Nagar?" I asked. "Give me a separate house here."

"You have picked up my gauntlet. In all my life I never remember saying anything to which you agreed. Until today I have listened to you; now at last I shall listen no more. I shall not let the boy suffer by dancing after you. I have given you five and a half years to consider things; now I give you till half-past five today

48

I shall take Dattu. If you do not let me, then I have other ways open to me." As he spoke his voice rose. In the end it reached the top of the scale, and I was afraid.

Having spoken, he went out for a walk. I felt as if I were in the midst of a blazing forest. I could see leaping flames from all sides. But I could not give up Dattu.

That evening a cart arrived to take us to the station. As we went, I was staring at Vithoba's temple, and repeating in my heart, "O God, a torch in either hand, willingly I leap into this river of trouble. Save me if thou wilt. Kill me if thou wilt. But do not throw me again on someone else's mercy." I was weeping steadily. Though Tilak was outwardly trying to preserve his stern air, he was by nature tender-hearted, full of love and grief. Dattu was only delighted to be in the cart with the joy of a train journey before him.

"Why behave like a lunatic?" said Tilak. "I shall never force you to become a Christian. I liked the religion, so I accepted it. If you like and accept it, it will make me very happy, but I shall not press you. All the things you have heard about this religion are completely false. You will be married off to no one. You will never have to cook meat. Who filled your head with such ideas? A Brahman's house is ready for you; pots, pans and everything. Also the house is near Pendse's. Why cry over nothing?"

I have experienced the truth of Tilak's words. During thirty-five years meat has never been cooked in our house.

Dr. Hume had taken the room for me, and furnished it. In place of the usual brass plates and bowls there were china cups, saucers and plates; instead of our big round spoons and ladles were knives, forks and spoons. I had never seen such things in my life before.

But already the landlord had heard that Tilak was a Christian and had said that he was not to come to the house. If he insisted, he must look for another house. It was never Tilak's nature to worry overmuch; he comforted himself with the thought that this was the will of God. Why should one worry? Without telling me, he sent me to Pendse's house to dine.

But here was no welcome for me. Their evening meal was over. No one would speak to me. The cook placed a dish before me on which there was one quarter of a cake of coarse *bajri* bread and some salt. No one even stood nearby. My own sister would have nothing to do with me, unless I agreed to leave Nagar and have nothing to do with Tilak.

Next day hope and despair had begun to play about me when Tilak arrived with two servants and a bullock-cart.

"I have found another house for you; the landlord will not keep you here. It is also a Brahman's; there is a Maratha woman to clean your pots, and a Brahman to carry your water." Dattu was fetched from Pendse's house, our things were put into the cart, and the three of us set off in a *tonga*. Even yet I had not set eyes on my sister.

We dined together, and Tilak went back to his own house near by; Dattu and I went to sleep happy in the thought that now we would have no more trouble. But in the morning our landlady sent us a message: "You must not use our lavatory." The very lavatory then was to be kept "holy"!

Then the Maratha woman, who had cleaned the pots once, betook herself off, and left word that she could clean them no more, or she would be put out of caste. The Brahman water-carrier was forbidden to draw water for us. He began to defend me: "My mistress puts on ceremonially clean clothes and worships the gods; why should you stop her water?" He was told that my husband was a Christian, and that was enough; he himself would have to undergo a ceremony of repentance and purification. The poor man had to make his expiation, and pay a fine of four or five rupees, and all because of me. There was no alternative but to move again.

"I will not go and live near Christians," I told Tilak.

"Then where will you go? Have you not seen for yourself the Brahman ways of the Brahmans? The guardian of knowledge is the Brahman, and this is a specimen of their knowledge. I am giving you no trouble; it is your own people that are casting you off. What can I do about that?"

We moved once more, this time into a compound from which all the Christians had been moved to make way for me. Here the missionaries came to see me, but no other Christians, because of Tilak's warning. But gradually they began to come to Tilak's rooms, where daily prayers, hymn-singing and Bible-reading were held; while in my part of the house there was the energetic worship of the gods and goddesses, *Ganpati* the elephant-headed god and the sacred *Tulsi* plant. He had servants, but I had none; I could not get a Maratha and would not have another caste. I had to do everything with my own hands.

Then plague broke out, and we must move again. Tilak was sent to Rahuri, twenty miles away, and there I lived for the first time entirely among Christians. There was one detached room in the compound, and here I did my cooking and worshipped my gods. I was still the daughter of Narayanrao Gokhale; as strictly as ever I observed all the Brahman laws to preserve my uncontaminated purity.

Next door to my room lived the *ayah* who was employed to look after a missionary's children. She was uneducated, but so well had she learned to study the feelings of others that only now do I realize the worth of her consideration for me. By degrees she began to do small things for me. "What harm if I sweep up the rubbish?" she would ask gently, and because of her sweet nature I began to let her; only the bringing of water and the cooking did I reserve for myself.

In the hot weather we moved to Mahabaleshwar for the language school.

There was a well close to our house, and on the first day of our stay I drew some water for Dattu and myself. Cold water, cool air and sweet food, our minds too at peace—no wonder we sat down to dinner with joy! But the mere mention of water brought, not only water into our eyes, but poison into our food. Tilak too had his pride and his obstinacy.

"You are not to draw and carry water yourself. It does not befit my condition. I shall put on a Brahman to do it."

My heart sank, for my experience in Nagar was still fresh in my memory. Where was a Brahman to be found tomorrow? and where had Tilak any time to look for one? All night my very dreams went out to look for water and returned empty at four in the morning. Though I played the perfect miser next day, by evening there was not enough left for Dattu and me.

"Drink this other water today," said Tilak; "from tomorrow I shall make a different arrangement."

"But once I have drunk it I have drunk it," said I. "What remedy is there for that?"

As usual I sat down to dinner, half choked with tears. A mouthful stuck in my throat.

"It is true religion to take care of your body," Tilak said. "Also the Hindu religion says that polluted water is purified by merely flowing four cubits distance. Drink this other water."

I raised the water drawn by a Mohammedan to my lips. Shutting my eyes tight, and with a wavering mind, I took a sip. It stayed in my mouth a brief moment, then it was promptly and violently ejected. I lay down on the spot shivering with rising fever. Tilak deeply regretted his obstinacy; what harm would there have been in my bringing water from the well in front of the house? He admitted his mistake.

Lying on my bed I washed the pillow with my tears. Secretly in my heart I continued to cry, "O God, what have I done today? What are my ancestors saying about me in heaven? What can I do to make amends for such a sin?" My mind was overwhelmed.

Yet all at once I felt as if a light was shining about me. That is not a form of speech; I truly experienced a brilliant light like that of the sun. My perturbation came to an end, and thoughts that had never before had entrance there began to whirl through my mind.

Tilak had great faith in God, and was praying without ceasing for me. Now he received the answer to his prayer. All the chains of caste distinction, that had bound my mind so tightly, burst and fell rattling down. It happened in the twinkling of an eye. At that time the ideas that came to me were so clear, that even now I can reproduce them on paper almost as they were.

Did God create different castes or did man? If God, then would He not have made also differences in mankind? Birth and death, flesh and bones, intelligence, the power to judge good and evil, joy, sorrow, these things do not all men have in common? And if amongst men God made high and low castes, then why did that same God not also arrange an order of castes in the animal world? A Brahman bull and a low-caste Sudra bull, a Vaishya (high-caste) crow and an untouchable crow? Do such differences appear among the birds and beasts? What is the difference between Brahman and Sudra? A Sudra has no bull's horns protruding from his skull. A Brahman is not born with the mark of his God-given greatness stamped on his forehead. If man and woman are of different castes, that's all. Enough, my caste distinctions were gone. From that day on I would hold all equal. The very roots of my caste pride had vanished. I would eat from anyone's hand, drink too from anyone's cup.

No sooner had I embarked on this train of thought than Ashammabai, the Christian woman who was staying with us, came and began her persuasions. "Rise up now, bring your water, and begin the cooking."

"I shall not bring the water, and I shall not do the cooking. You do it for me, and I shall eat it."

She could not understand the purpose behind my words, and called Tilak. I told him plainly that I was not going to cook.

"You are upsetting yourself about nothing," he said. "I shall never again say a word to you, either about the water or the cooking. Do as you please."

But I was not to be moved from my decision. "What I tell you, I tell you in all sincerity. I am not saying it out of temper."

When Tilak was once convinced that I meant what I said, he was exceedingly happy. He said in English, "Thank God" and began to pray. Ashammabai cooked the meal, and with great joy we dined together.

It was the first time in my life that I had ever eaten anything from the hand of another caste.

Tilak now started married life anew. There was no more question about eating and drinking. Though I had not become a Christian, and had no intention of doing so, all my caste prejudices had evaporated. Our two different régimes were now merged into one. Tilak put no obstacle in the way of my idol-worship, and I was always present at his prayers.

A couple of months after returning from Mahabaleshwar, on Dr. Ballantine's invitation we went for a few days to Rahuri. We were given a little house, where every morning and evening there was Bible reading, prayers and hymn-singing. The hymns sung were composed by Tilak. The neighbours always gathered for prayers, and the group would repeat those Bible verses they liked. Dattu and I were Hindus, nevertheless we were always present at Tilak's prayers, and I began to like them. It was a new experience for me to commune with God in my heart. Hearing the Bible read again and again, I grew familiar with it.

It was a Saturday, and a group had gathered for the usual prayers. All the Christians present repeated a verse of Scripture. It was Dattu's turn; he said: "God is love." Then came my turn and I repeated the verse: "God, have mercy upon me, a sinner."

"God will never have mercy on you," said Tilak.

"Why not?"

"If being bound to me by promise you desert me, what can I think of you? Even so, if you live apart from Christ to whom you are devoted, how can God be pleased with such deception? How can He have mercy on you?"

Prayers being over, I went out. I told no one where I was going, but made straight for Dr. Ballantine's bungalow, and knocked on his door. He was very astonished to see me.

"Well, Lakshmibai, have you come alone?"

"Sahib, baptize me tomorrow."

"Now, Lakshmibai, you have no knowledge of the Bible yet. You will have to study the Christian religion for at least five or six months."

"I have a good knowledge of the Christian religion now. I want to be baptized tomorrow."

"But why all this hurry?"

"Never mind, if you do not intend to baptize me, say so plainly."

"But there will be questions put to you, and you will have to answer at the time."

"I know nothing about that, tell me if you are going to baptize me or not, or I shall go."

"You had better go for the present. I cannot give an answer now."

"Sahib, tomorrow is Sunday. My baptism, Dattu's and Houshi's (the famine-child adopted by the Tilaks) must be performed tomorrow. Even though I pass in no Scripture examination, my faith is in Christ. Why should I lie?"

Dr. Ballantine and I prayed there and then, and our baptism was arranged for the morrow. He told me a story: There was a man; an unexpected guest came to his house at night. The host had nothing to give him to eat, so he went to a neighbour and brought back something.

I did not unravel the story at the time and later forgot it altogether, but today as I write I begin to appreciate the reference (St. Luke 11 : 5–8). The baptisms were arranged, and in that happy knowledge I went home. Tilak was filled with joy when he heard the whole story from my lips.

56

Before my baptism I was examined. A pastor from somewhere was visiting Rahuri. He was a most kindly man and old enough to be my father. He sat beside me prompting me with the answers to the questions on the Bible, and I repeated his answers to the examiners. I refused to accept baptism at the hands of a foreign missionary, and expressed my desire to be baptized by the pastor of the congregation, the Reverend Waniramji Bapuji Ohol. So I, Dattu and Houshi were baptized in the church at Rahuri. That day I was also received into full membership and was given permission to partake of Holy Communion.

CHAPTER FIVE

SERVANTS OF THE POOR

On becoming Christian, or rather on being caught in the current of Christianity, I took a Mahar (outcaste) girl into my house, as if she were my own. Later when we were at Nagar Tilak adopted a Mahar boy called Bhikaji.

God granted another of my desires. For ten years after my last child there had been no baby in the house; now God gave me a baby to be called my own. We called her Tara—a star. We both loved her more than our own lives, and together we brought her through her babyhood with much trouble and difficulty.

Only four or five days after her coming she looked like leaving us. Immediately we were delivered from that anxiety, it was time to leave for Mahabaleshwar, where Tilak used to spend the hot weather teaching Marathi to European and American missionaries. But for once his pilgrimage was neglected. Tara was three weeks old, and would survive neither the cold of Mahabaleshwar nor the heat of Nagar, so we decided to take her to Wai at the foot of the hills.

Because the baby was so small and the train was crowded, Dr. Hume reserved a second class compartment for us. Each of us sat in his or her own seat. Only Tilak kept moving from one to another, and climbing from the lower to the upper sleeping berths.

"Do sit still in one place, please," I begged.

He thought I was very old-fashioned. I believed in not moving from my seat once I was in it, and I would go and sit at the station for four hours in fear of missing the train. I would send a wire when someone was at the point of death, but not otherwise. Naturally I thought Tilak should keep to his own seat in the train, but he would have none of it. Finally in leaping from one berth to another his sleek pate encountered the shining lamp, and both had a glimpse of paradise. A stream of blood began to flow from his head. The lamp was in smithereens.

Down below, the children were asleep and the tiny pieces of glass were scattered over their faces. On the one hand I was afraid they would wake up and the glass would go in their eyes, on the other hand Tilak was bathed in blood. He however was perfectly calm, as if nothing whatsoever had happened. He went into the bathroom and poured cold water over his head, which stopped the bleeding, but there was a very big cut left. With great care I picked and brushed the glass off the children's faces, then wiped the blood off the carriage floor with the end of my sari.

"How are you?"

"What is wrong with me?"

"What do you mean, 'What is wrong with me?'"

"Tush! Such things must be. They add zest to life."

"We shall be fined for breaking the lamp."

"If we are, we can pay the fine. Will worrying about it make the fine less, if there is one? And will a wound be healed by anxiety?"

We had no fine nor anything to pay. Tilak's body was as wiry as his mind was vigorous.

One day it was raining. Dattu and Houshi had both gone off to school. Tilak was taking a class in theology, so I was alone in the house. I was sitting near the door cleaning the rice when a girl came to beg. She was only a skeleton of bones, her head looking as big as a basket with her uncombed hair, and no substance in her body. The last vestige of vitality was cupped in her hungry eyes. Wearing a handsbreadth of worn-out rag to preserve her modesty she came and stood by the door in the rain, a tin can in her hand. There was a fresh weal of a wound across her face.

I took her into the house, then began to question her.

"Would you rather beg or live in a house?"

"Beg."

"Would you stay with me?"

"Yes."

"What relations have you?"

"No one. Everyone has left me. My village is far away."

By now I had made up my mind to keep her. I gave her a bath, and provided her with one of Houshi's saris. Even with so little, what a transformation was wrought in her appearance. When Tilak and the children came home in the evening they were very amused.

"What is this?"

"This is a picture of the famine. I have taken her in."

"What for? We have Houshi, God has given us our Tara, and. . . ."

"And this is Daya whose name means pity. I have had pity on her, and God too has had mercy on her."

"All right, never mind."

In a little while some of the neighbouring Christian women came to see us.

"Sahib, do you know whose child this is?"

"No. Why?"

"Well, she is a Mang, one of the lowest castes."

"Well?"

"Do you think nothing of it?"

"Nothing; why? Mang, Mahar, Brahman, all are the same."

"You have outstripped us. We cannot go as far as that." So saying the women left. They avoided our house for several days. Tilak however from now on began to employ Mang, Mahar, and all the low castes for servants in the house.

The day after Daya arrived, an aged Mang woman came to fight with Tilak about her. From out of their vituperations the following information could be gathered. In the course of her begging, Daya had come to this old woman, who had given her shelter. Daya would bring back what alms she earned, and the woman let her stay in her house. They both lived off the proceeds of Daya's begging.

"How long has she been staying with you?"

"Eight days."

"From that you establish a claim over her? And who raised that scar on her cheek?"

"I do not know."

"You lie, hag! Tell the truth or I shall send you to prison to grind grain."

Wavering between truth and falsehood she confessed that, because the girl did not bring enough home, she had branded her cheek with an iron. Now indeed Tilak was angry, and the woman fled, never to show her face again.

After she was gone, we learned a little more about her. We found that she gathered young girls, and sold them. In truth God had had pity on Daya in sending her to us. She and Houshi went to school together, and we had not so much trouble as a blade of grass from either of them. They neither stole nor lied nor did anything objectionable. They behaved in the house

61

as if they were our own. My fear that they would spit in the house and scatter leavings and rubbish about proved absolutely unfounded. They did as they saw us do. And they became quite good cooks.

Presently the famine began to take on a fearful aspect. In addition the Mission suffered a loss, or something of the sort, and they turned some children out of the boarding-school. This started an uproar throughout the whole town. The children had no place to which they could go. Tilak came to me and said, "These twenty-two children will die of hunger. What can be done?"

That day we had in hand a balance of one rupee, and one and a quarter *seers* of *jowari* in our meal bin. Nevertheless we had another large balance, which proved more than enough; it was our faith in God. Bowing our heads we prayed from our hearts to the Almighty, then we made a vow to each other to make no difference between our food and that of these children. We too would eat whatever black bread we gave to them.

We called Dattu to us, and drawing him close said, "My son, today your starving brothers are wandering over the countryside. We are going to bring them home. You will have to eat what they eat. Will you do it?"

"I shall both eat and drink with them. I shall never grumble," he replied; and he kept his promise faithfully. We sent Houshi and Daya to a school in Poona, and the boys came to stay with us.

The famine which had already been ferocious now began to beggar all description. Not only could food not be obtained, there began to be a shortage of water too. From the year 1895 Tilak maintained a staff of servants who were never changed; among them was our water-carrier.

"Though in the bazaar I sell one buffalo-skin of water for a rupee," he said, "I shall supply your water at the usual rate. Only grant me this concession, that I may bring it as I am able." He began to bring the water at one or two in the morning. A padlock was put on the back door, and the key was given to him, and with the utmost faithfulness he brought two skins filled to the brim. Nearly all the household pots were earthenware; the place was stacked with them like a potter's house, and these and all other vessels, even to the drinking glasses, he filled. By dint of purchasing on credit, and this happy arrangement which was a reward of Tilak's own generous heart, the appalling famine was not so much felt in our house. Cloth was bought on credit, and clothes sewn for the children. Coats, trousers, hats, shirts and all their outfit were made on the spot. A large quantity of coir was procured and twenty-two mattresses sewn. Naturally with them appeared a whole family of mats, pillows and blankets. Each child was given a separate plate and drinking vessel.

Bhikaji also got his share of all these things in proportion to his age. Everyone was very fond of him, but he was for ever being belaboured by Tilak on account of his intense stupidity. Was it not Tilak's good intention to turn him into a learned scholar? Was he not nicknamed *Shastri-bawa*, Doctor of Scripture? And he could not learn so much as the first lesson—not the first words of Sanskrit, *Ramah, Ramao!* Wherefore every day, before he had even brushed his teeth, he got a taste of Tilak's hand. First his Sanskrit lesson, a little gingering up, then Bhikaji's cantata, then Tilak's fury, and then the last scene of all in which everyone appeared with efforts at conciliation; thus a state of opera became our daily entertainment.

Tilak sent some of these twenty-two boys to school, some of them to the printing-press, and some elsewhere to learn a trade. The boys themselves began to look much improved, living happily and contentedly in their new home. They behaved very well with us, and neither stole nor lied; among them all lived Dattu.

Grinding from time immemorial has been women's work, but the boys agreed to share it, and so expenses were kept down. If any of the boys fell ill, I washed their clothes myself, otherwise the sweeper would have to be paid to do it. That money bought our vegetables.

But another disaster overtook us in the midst of all this love and happiness. Just as I always quarrelled with Tilak over money—at our wedding he bound a garland of care about my neck, and I a garland of carelessness about his—so now Dr. Hume blamed both of us, and especially me, for being extravagant. He was not in the least pleased that we should take charge of the boys. He was right in a way. By the first of every month not even the following month's salary remained. He considered that we were only involving ourselves in difficulties by continuing charity when there was such a lack of funds. Of course this dispute arose out of his unfeigned love for Tilak, so any anger we may have felt over his interference in our affairs was shortlived.

The phrase, "Now, brother", was always on Dr. Hume's lips, when he spoke out of the depths of exasperation. He now set to work to goad us into giving up the children.

"Now, brother, your expenses are far too heavy You will find yourselves in difficulties."

"Sahib, how can you say that? 'The mother will not

feed her children, and the father will not let them beg.' "

"Now, sister, I do not understand what you are saying."

"I say that you will not make arrangements for them, nor will you let us take care of them. Is that fair?"

"All right, brother, I shall go now. Think over this matter well. I shall too."

We thought long over it. "To what a state of weakness have these missionaries reduced us," said Tilak. "As if missionaries had a monopoly in helping others! 'Is anyone in need? show them the missionary's bungalow.' Done! That's all the help we Christian people can give. They have sown this habit. Come what may, we shall not let these children go until suitable provision has been made for them."

In this state of indecision we kept the children for eleven months. When I heard from outside the compound one of Tilak's hymns, with some of its words turned topsyturvy, I knew that Dr. Hume had come to plead with us again; he always came singing. At last he sent me a letter: "I have arranged to take all your children into my boarding-school, and I shall see that they will not be sent away again."

We were both very sad, but also very relieved. That day sweetened rice was prepared for the boys. Till well after midnight we all sat talking, and as we talked "the floods of Ganges and Yamune came upon us"—we wept. In the end Tilak prayed, and we all went to bed.

We had incurred a debt of five hundred rupees for these children. "By God's grace it is next to nothing," said Tilak. "We have done all this with a clear conscience, and without a doubt God will assist us to repay."

So indeed it turned out. Some American gentleman gave Tilak a cheque for five hundred rupees the next day; before the boys had left our threshold, the cloth merchant and the grain merchant had their money in hand, and we were free.

CHAPTER SIX

LOWER YET—AND HIGHER

Plague broke out in Nagar, and a plague camp was
opened. Tilak would not be inoculated, nor allow
Tara to be; and she caught the disease from a rat
which died beside her pillow. So the whole family,
en at that time, was moved into the camp.—Ed.]

It was a pitch-dark night and we had no lantern.
The bumping of the cart, the babbling of the child,
and the beating of my heart furnished the accompaniment for our journey, till out of the bumps and
hollows we reached the camp. Tilak came forward
to greet us.

"We have been allocated three huts, one for cooking,
one for Tara, and one where I can sit and write," he
said.

The doctor came and examined Tara. She had a
temperature of 105 degrees.

"You must not stay near the child," he said. "You
will get plague. This woman will sit beside her."

"Why?" I said. "Who was Tara sitting near when
she got plague? And even though I sit elsewhere, why
should I not get it? And if I am to leave her, why
should this paid woman stay with her rather than I?"
The doctor remained silent.

Tilak brought us all something to eat, but what
meat and drink! left-over *jowari* bread from the
morning, and water cold as ice from an earthen pitcher.

It was November, and bitterly cold. At top and bottom of the hut walls was a handsbreadth left open—for ventilation! The huts were all built of corrugated iron. At night they were so cold that everyone inside was likely to be frozen to death. On three sides were ill people. They groaned, the corrugated iron rattled, then some delirious patient would climb over the iron walls, and drop with a thud into the adjoining room. There were no floors; one's feet were bruised with stones and gravel; there was no food for one's stomach, and no sleep for one's eyes. I thought to myself, if there were a hell anywhere it was here. The patients and their relatives too were crying and quarrelling; some were really ill, and some just shouting in terror.

At first there were no proper arrangements in the camp at all. We were given ten days' rations of uncooked rice and fuel, and Daya did the cooking. There was a common thermometer and medicine glass; when I described the night scene to the doctor, he gave belladonna and the nights grew quieter. Ten per cent of the patients survived. After a fortnight we were told that there was no hope for Tara.

I abandoned hope, and laid her down. I made a hot poultice, and warming some castor oil, milk and sugar together I poured it somehow down her throat. I placed the brazier near her feet, wrapped her up well in a blanket, and then said to her, "Now die if you like; let me not think I have left anything undone."

Leaving her alone and closing the door, I went far out into the country. When I was quite alone I knelt down, and cried aloud in prayer, "O God our Father, let the child live. She is not mine, she is Thine. Thou gavest her to me, and I have cared for her. If it be Thy will take her away

68

If she recovers I shall nurse the plague patients here."

So saying I lifted up my voice and wept my heart out. When I returned I had no courage to open the door. But the moment it was open, Tara called to me, "Mama, where are you? Where is Papa?" I was so relieved, I longed to pick her up; but reminding myself that it might have a bad effect on her heart, I fled to Tilak's hut. Tilak and a group of others were sitting praying. He thought I had come to bring the news of her end. I said laughing, and over and over again, "Baby is asking for you." He could not believe it. At last we went together to Tara's hut. As soon as she saw him, she said, "Why did you leave me, Papa? bring me some mangoes."

We left the hut eighteen days after our arrival.

Tilak's reading, writing and prayers were continued as usual all this time. He used to say, "O God, I do not as yet see why Thou hast brought this calamity upon us. I only know that there must be some purpose of Thine in it. Give me the wisdom to understand Thy will."

One day there was an argument in camp about the milk. Hearing voices raised, Tilak went over to the spot. "Let me see the note-book," he said.

"Sahib, you would not understand it."

Therewith Tilak snatched the book and began to examine it. The figure entered was large, and the milk before him but little. Tilak returned to me to say he had received the answer to his prayer; he now understood God's purpose in permitting that Tara should get plague. There were not enough trustworthy men in the place. The milk entered in the account was three times the amount delivered.

"I have made a resolution," said Tilak, "that

I shall stay here and render whatever service I can to those patients. Are you ready?"

"Yes, I am ready," I replied.

God gave us great courage and big hearts. He gave us the mind of one who fears no disease, who cares not what filthy work he does, the very mind of a sweeper! That which even a mother will tire of doing, a sweeper will do daily for us his ungrateful brethren.

With all our heart we two set to work.

A hut was built for us near the camp, but now the ration of uncooked rice and fuel was stopped, and water had to be brought by the water-carrier. All against my will, I took in two babies whose mothers had died of plague. Tilak and I did whatever fell to be done for the patients. We looked after their food and drink and medicines. We washed their faces and gave them sponge-baths. People of every religion and every caste were there, and on hearing that we were working among them, the fear of the camp grew less, and more and more plague patients began to come.

In the camp there was a man of Teli caste, who was put under lock and key. No one had courage so much as to go and give him a drink of water. As soon as we undertook the responsibility, we introduced a new nurse, Jaibai, a Christian who put her whole heart into her work. On the first day after she arrived, we went to the Teli's hut, only to find a guard on the door.

"Do not go in, *bai*," he said. "This man is positively dangerous."

"Let him be dangerous or anything else, it is our duty to give him milk and medicine. Unlock the door."

"Be careful, won't you? He may attack you."

And truly, as soon as the door was opened he leaped upon us. As he approached I struck him violently in the face. Who knows what happened to him, he bowed himself at my feet and took his milk and medicine without a word.

In time of need servants can take advantage. One day all the sweepers suddenly struck work for higher pay. For two days Tilak and I did all the scavenger's work. On the third day corpses had to be removed. Tilak girded up his loins; I tucked in the loose end of my sari. The sweepers sat with folded hands while we lifted two and placed them in the cart. At last they were abashed. They came running and said, "Sahib, flog our backs, but not our stomachs."

"I have never said you should receive no more salary," said Tilak, "only that in such a crisis it does not do credit to your humanity to put such people into a predicament. We shall certainly endeavour to procure a rise in salary for you. It is not right that you should cause obstruction when these, your brothers, are dying. I shall do what I can about your pay, but if ever afterwards you should repeat this, understand that you get no more help from me."

When Tilak first undertook the service of the plague-stricken patients, some people said that his daughter's plague had proved a profitable thing for him, that he was raking in easy money. Others said, "See how he labours for the poor." Tilak himself said:

> The world's a game,
> With praise and blame
> To bait the trap
> On Folly's lap.
> The trap touch not;
> For praise laugh not;
> Weep not for blame;
> Weep not for blame.

71

The plague-stricken inmates began to get better. The death-rate came down to ten per cent. Everyone's photograph was taken. The Civil Surgeon gave Tilak a certificate, expressing at the same time great gratitude. Tilak put it into a file for letters, but it ended its days somewhere among the waste paper.

In all Tilak's life I found one constant factor—he cared neither for praise nor blame in the pursuit of his duty; he thought absolutely nothing of fame. Saying, "Write my life as it has been," he would add, "In no wise cover up my faults." One thing more was that his life, so filled with high ideals, had an immediate effect on other people; otherwise it would have been impossible for Narayanrao Gokhale's daughter to be ready to undertake cheerfully and enthusiastically the work of a sweeper. Had not my father for a whole life-time scrubbed and washed himself and all his household, because he imagined a mere drop of water from a low-caste Mahar's mouth had touched his body? Would I, this father's daughter, ever run to do the lowest work in a plague hospital?

If there be anything in that to be praised, then it is Tilak who must be praised. He was in these things my teacher. He led the way, and my part was only to run boldly along it with my eyes shut. If any portion of the credit be due to me, it is merely in that without wavering I went forward fearlessly in the trail he had blazed. So!

CHAPTER SEVEN

TILAK AND THE GRACE OF GOD

Tilak was "Ra, Ra,"—the Marathi equivalent of Mister. He became Reverend. This is the story of it.

Tilak began to think he would prefer to leave mission-paid employment, and decided not to do God's work for a salary. He made up his mind to collect volunteers and found a society. He sent in his resignation and began to gather his "volunteers" about him. One volunteer encamped in our house at Rahuri, with all his family, and it was a family of six. Next an assembly of four farm servants, the night watchman and the progeny of his three wives were all gathered round us.

Dr. Hume did not oppose Tilak's new profession, but, knowing that "husband a mendicant" implies "wife a martyr", he persuaded the Tract Society to give him work at a hundred rupees a month, which meant that he was working for nothing for the mission at Rahuri, and yet things were going fairly smoothly, though the hundred rupees had a hundred claims upon them.

Many enquirers about Christianity came to him, and he began to say that anyone having a call from God should baptize those who might be ready; that it was not necessary to be ordained in order to baptize; and without title he performed some baptisms. This action gave some people a great shock, but not even the great God Brahma could prevent him from embarking on anything once he was convinced it was right; so now many people were in a dilemma. Tilak never cared much what people thought. If anyone came to him to be baptized, instead of sending him to some "Reverend" he would perform the ceremony himself, and be done with it. And even with that he was not content; he would argue about it.

Who knows what was decided in the Church Council? but it was arranged that Tilak's ordination should take place in Rahuri.

While we were living in Rahuri (about 1905–6) Tilak wrote a great many religious poems. One day when he was out for a walk with some Christian friends, they passed a Hindu procession singing and dancing; and Tilak, feeling there was too much Western influence in the Christian services, in singing and form of worship, composed some of his most famous hymns—"O Christ, if I leave Thee, whither shall I go?" "Christ my tender Teacher", and many others. Out of 682 in the Marathi hymn-book 254 are by him. Filled with the same spirit of devotion are two books, *The Lord's Prayer* and *Bhajanasangraha*. Tilak used to say that he first became Christian intellectually, and not until some ten years later did he become Christian in spirit; it would not be wrong to say these were the days of his second conversion, and the disturbance of his spirit is reflected in his poems. His natural pride vanished to be replaced by a spirit of dependence upon God. His eyes would fill with tears when he sang the following hymn written in 1906:

At last my Lord and King, to Thy dear feet I cling.
All lost this life of mine without the light of Thine.
I saw my own self stand the first at Christ's right
    hand,

In pride of strength and grace. Ah, now before Thy
    face
That pride is low as dust. No more myself I trust.
Myself was my own foe, that would not let me know
How far I strayed from God, how dark the path I
    trod.
The name I bore was Thine; the will I served was
    mine.
I have no wisdom's light, no knowledge, power or
    might.
O Christ, to Thee I bow, my all in all art Thou.

Once the barriers of thought were raised round
Tilak's mind, he had no more care for the outside
world. He was wise, I was witty, yet his wisdom was
no barrier to me, and my bantering no burden to him.

In these ten years, while we lived at Rahuri and then
in Nagar, happiness and amusement had the first
place. Tilak was a keen dice player, quick to play and
quick to quarrel. We would all lose our tempers, but
still be laughing. His belongings were always being
lost; "lost" means that he never put them in their
proper places, never looked in the proper place, and
would not allow anyone to hunt with him. Teeth,
matchbox, hat, spectacles and belt were forever
evading his hand.

Especially when he was due at a class, or leaving
to give a lecture in some village, his boots and stockings,
hat, umbrella, collar, belt and sandals would all play
hide-and-seek with him, and round him we would
dance a jing-a-ring. Many a time he had to go without
his hat, or in place of his belt the rope had to be loosed
from the calf's neck and tied round his waist!

"No one looks after me. Everyone is taken up with
their own affairs. No one cares for me," he used to say,

and then we would run with one accord to wait upon him. Once in this way his teeth were lost. What a fuss!

"The dog has gone off with my teeth," he said. "Or else the mice have hidden them under the stack of wood you have built up here. Take it all away, and fling it outside. What a toil she makes of house-keeping!" No sooner said than done! All the logs for firewood began to chase each other round the compound.

Another day his hat was lost. It was on the peg, and a coat had been hung on top of it. Tilak was called to go out, and in his flurry put on another coat, and then began to search for his hat. To begin with he flung the first coat down on the floor, and with it hidden underneath went the hat. Then, as in that sacrifice of snakes in olden days when coil upon coil fell into the pot of fire, so now all the clothes in all the cup-boards in the house began to fall one upon another into the heap. Bedding, mats, blankets were all swept up in company, and added to the rising pile.

"Go, go and call Manjulabai. What is she doing? Look for my hat. What is the use of you people? Can you be turned into a vegetable? Find my hat for me at once."

"But, Papa" (schoolboys, servants and all called him that), "may it not be *under* this pile?" After which i was not possible to say a word more, and Manjulaba went into his office, ostensibly to hunt for the hat and came out only when she saw him departing bare headed.

When Tilak was out of the way we lifted up the clothes, and there was the hat!

In the year 1916 Dattu passed his B.A., and planned after further study, to become a lawyer. At this time Tilak's nature began to change with increasing rapidity. From earliest childhood there had been a constant ferment in his mind; he felt there was no use in remaining as one was. To the last moment he desired to be something better, and at last gained the victory over the very great faults within himself.

Now he determined to leave Nagar and his teaching, and settle in Satara. Years before, he had decided to write an epic, and had taken himself off to begin the *Christayan*, a life of Christ in poetry. Now the desire to sit down and finish it had taken hold of his mind. His nature had never allowed him to do this; he knew so many people in Nagar, and so many people knew him to be in Nagar, that the numbers coming to call upon him began to increase enormously, and once a discussion on some favourite topic started, hours would go by without consideration. In the quiet of Satara he might complete his work.

Dr. Hume used to do everything possible for Tilak; and so we were given a big bungalow to live in. *Christayana Ashram* was the name Tilak gave to it, and he had a name-plate made and put up. Our living was of the poorest as before, but now it was in a large and handsome building! There was neither furniture nor furnishings anywhere; everything was bare, and all doors stood open as in an ascetic's monastery. People could come and go as they liked. There we lived for the last three years of Tilak's life.

Tilak was the editor of *Dnyanodaya*, the weekly Christian paper; he had a clerk who helped in this task, and also copied out the *Christayan* as it was written. Tilak asked one of his family, who had a good voice, to teach me "Do, Ray, Me"; and sometimes he would sit down and practise with me, because we planned to go on tour singing *kirtans*.

Tilak had come to Satara to write the *Christayan*;

77

but once more the epic was left in the lurch. There was no lack of other occupations; he founded two societies, and travelled widely. My reproaches only earned a scolding.

"How much do you understand about it? An epic is a work of inspiration. Is poetry ever written to order?"

He was invited to lecture to the Christians at Dindigul in the Madras Presidency, and saw there one astounding thing which was completely unknown among the Christians of Maharashtra. These people of Madras, though they had become Christians, had not immediately thrown off the burden of untouchability, but clutched it to their bosoms and carried it along with them. Some people sat inside the church, and some, the untouchable Christians, sat outside.

It was not in Tilak's nature to put up with this, and one day when he arrived he sat down among the people outside. He would not even turn his head to look at those inside, but began his address from where he sat. One by one the people inside, being shamed, began to come out and sit down. After this Tilak made it a rule that he would not speak in any place where such distinctions were made.

Tilak had felt, practically from the time he had become a Christian, that he did not want to be a paid mission agent. Once or twice he had ceased to accept the salary and continued the same work without pay. Now, however, he was about to undertake a very great and different task, the preparation for which meant the complete renunciation of mission employment. From Rahuri on 1 September, 1917, he published this letter:

"A Humble Statement
"For the sake of my country and for the sake of

78

Christ's *Darbar* I can no more be bound to any human institution in any way, except by the ties of love and service. From now on all my desire must be towards, and all my profit in, Christ and His Gospel. Therefore I obey the voice of God and from henceforth I am no servant, doing the work of a mission or any other human institution for pay. I am become a Christian ascetic, which means, not one devoid of all desire and passion, but an ascetic following the path of love. From henceforth I must endeavour to be and do what God, who is Spirit, tells me. Those who love Christ, India and me should intercede for me before the Mercy-seat of God, the Father of us all. This is the help I ask."

He renounced his salary and began to wear a beggar's robe. He possessed only two, which he washed himself. Now there were no servants in the house. He himself did everything, from lighting the fire to plastering the floor with cow-dung.

One Christian gentleman asked if his adoption of an ascetic's life meant the renouncing of family ties.

"To live dependent on a beggar's bowl! Perish the life of shame! No Christian ascetic will ever do that. I am become a mendicant because I am prepared to serve India. I want the wages for that service, but just enough for that service. If anyone should lay down before me a million rupees out of pity for my family, I would not take it. If the world gives me for the price of my service only enough to fill my own stomach then I shall remain hungry, and lay the food before my family. If the world decides to give me enough to support ten, I shall sit down with my family and eat a bite, and return to the world what is left over of the world's. We consider the plague that has scourged

79

our country a terrible thing, but there is a more terrible plague for ever at our heels. The name of that plague is *Begging*, either at home or abroad. There is no need for the Christian ascetic to add to the already innumerable beggars."

We were always poor; and Tilak always prayed to God to keep him so: "I do not want money." *My* prayer used to be, "I do not want to be in debt, O Lord." God answered both of us, by changing our attitude to money. Tilak's was expressed in one of his poems:

"May money never bring pain to hand or heart!"

In answer to my prayer, Tilak gave up getting into debt. He stopped borrowing altogether, and we were neither debtor nor creditor to anyone.

Even so it was my nature to grumble. I used to say: "You never can tell. One needs a little money in case anything happens."

"Will He not now provide for us, who made provision before we were even born? What is to be gained by worrying?" Only in shedding tears was Tilak a perfect miser; he had made over that whole contract to me.

CHAPTER EIGHT

SAFE HOME AT LAST

The last year of Tilak's life was in many ways worth ten others. He used to say our country would never attain to its true greatness without bringing the teaching of Christ into practice, or until men were regarded as more sacred than books or cults. His prayer to Christ was: "Let my soul be a mirror that will reflect Thee to the world. Live Thou in my thought, live Thou in my speech, live Thou in all my deeds, O most Holy." This train of thought made him dissatisfied with the conditions about him. He said a Christian must be like Christ, and an Indian Christian in every way like an Eastern Christ.

He began to make surpassing efforts to be so himself. More than ten years earlier, he had said: "O Lord, I am still far short of Thee; I have not freed myself in the least from the debts of my brothers and sisters. O Saviour of the unholy, I shall ever remain indebted to Thee." Many of the faults with which he had been born thus slowly disappeared, and in this last year it would be no exaggeration to say they vanished completely. Not once, when he was insulted, was he seen to lose his temper, as he used to do; but his rage was many a time transformed into righteous indignation.

By the grace of God there were plenty of people in our house. Different castes, different religions, different ways of thought, gathered under our roof; but all were of one heart and mind. Some were thinking about Christianity, some had already thought about it, and some had accepted it.

Twice every day there were meetings for hymn singing and choruses. Neighbours, people from the town, and sometimes passers by would come in and sit down. From want of money Tilak began to wear a saffron robe made from an old *dhoti*; he would stand among us while we sang together, with cymbals or castanets and the beating of a drum as accompaniment. Sometimes he would fasten jingling ornaments to his feet and dance in his abandonment. He and his audience would rise to that state of ecstasy when "body is forgotten in union with God" and they would continue their singing indefinitely.

Not all the missionaries approved; a disciplinarian cannot be expected to get on with a man guided only by inspiration. One such was forever locking the school in which services were held, so that Tilak should not preach.

"Let the building be never so simple," said Tilak, "but let it be your own. Build a church with your own hands; live on one meal a day, endure privation, but build your own church. How long are you going to drink water from another's hands? How much longer are you to remain like a cat with its nose in a dish? It is a century since you became Christian; are you still to remain children only able to crawl?"

To the missionaries he said, "How long are you going to spoon-feed us? Let us stand on our own feet. Do not interfere; let us try. Let us battle with the waves, let us die, but let us learn to swim."

Yet except for one, no Christian man nor missionary ever tried to harm Tilak; on the contrary, all behaved with the utmost friendliness.

One night, when Tilak felt that his death was not

82

ar away, he sat up and wrote his will. As you will wonder what kind of a will he made when he did not possess a farthing, I give part of it below:

"Life is not to be measured by time but by the performance of useful work. It is better that a man should die than that he should do no useful service. Everywhere in this world, I see but two things— Beauty and Ugliness. I delight in Beauty, therefore I have loved it. My only reason for loving Christ so deeply is that He is the essence of Beauty. He Himself is the image of this Beauty. No one can truly love this Beauty in the hope of heaven or the fear of hell. Love knows no desire. I delight in Beauty, therefore have I loved Him sincerely.

"If it is the wish of my friends and relatives to put up a tombstone over the spot where my body is laid, on that stone should be carved the line, *How imperfect am I, even yet, O Lord.* . . .

"No one knows when his calling will come from God, and no one should waste time in futile thought about it. I shall never describe the calling of God as 'Death', because it is to be called of God, God's calling. It is an awakening to new life. . . . My remains should be placed in the cemetery at Nagar; and in the Theological College there, a picture of myself and one of Dr. Hume should be hung side by side, and under Dr. Hume's should be written the words 'He took care of', and under mine 'this man'."

Just five months before his death, in a letter to Mrs. Lee, Dr. Hume's daughter, he sent the following messages:

"1. To India: Follow Jesus.

"2. To my Christian Brothers and Sisters: Your life is in Christ, your life is in Him and nothing else.

"3. To Missionaries: Cease to be fathers and mothers, be real brothers and sisters. Know how to appreciate, trust people, and take the place of India's revered saints.

"4. To all: I lived as a friend, and died as a friend of all, and I am still both here and hereafter."

He suggested that, if a monument is to be raised over his grave, no name should be written on it, but only "Someone that in right earnest loved Jesus and his countrymen."

Tilak had no fear of death, though he longed to finish the *Christayan*. "A mother knows how long to let her child play outside; when he is tired of playing she lifts him up, and takes him in beside her, and makes him rest. God does the same. If not today, tomorrow He will take each in his turn. We should look forward eagerly to that day."

At the beginning of July, 1919, he went into hospital in Bombay. After five days Tara compelled me to go with her to the hospital. There I found Tilak lying, writing still. While he was wrestling with Death he produced an article for *Dnyanodaya* and some hymns. It was Tara who contrived that I should speak with Tilak for the last time, and that I should see him while he was still conscious. "I am now better. I shall soon be quite well. Do not worry. . . . Guess which is my favourite hymn:

What though by foes oppressed I stand,
Besieged, hemmed in on either hand;
What though their patience, courage, tower
Like hills unbent to mortal power;

84

What cause hath he to flinch or fear
Whose Father, God Most High, stands near?

My foe presents before my eyes
All griefs and fleshly agonies,
And still behind me brandisheth
His ancient arms, old age and death.
Weak shield, frail helm, and frailest sword
'Gainst him whose Father is the Lord."

Four days later he died. Dattu too was gravely ill,
but just in time he was able to get to the hospital.
Tilak saw his son at last, and was able to fill his eyes
with the sight of him. He could not speak, but pointed
to his face with his finger. Dattu dropped a spoonful
of water into his mouth, and then Tilak breathed his
last. The morning song he used to sing every day
came into my mind:

Rise, rise, oh my Soul
Praise the Lord of Day and Night.
In the beginning of the new path of Life
Sing the glory of God.

According to Tilak's orders, black was completely
banished from his funeral, and there was no question
of a black or white hearse, because the company
insisted on carrying the coffin on their shoulders.
The hymn selected by the people to sing during
the funeral procession was Tilak's own. Though
sixteen years have passed since then (1935), I think
I can hear the words and tune resounding in my ears
yet. This is the hymn:

What fear hath he whose Master is the Lord,

Whose heart and mind can form no alien thought,
Who speaketh of the Lord his God alone,
Who liveth in the world to bless the world,
But owneth no allegiance to the world?
His poverty is here his sole reward,
But all the wealth of heaven is his to hold.
His body is his own, but therein dwells
Not his own soul, but lo, the Soul of Christ.
Beneath his conquering foot lie agonies
Of heart and flesh, and even death dies there.

The following is a selection of some of the best-known of Tilak's poems.

FROM THE *CHRISTAYAN*
(translated by the Rev. J. C. Winslow)

Ah! with a tide I cannot stem
    Break forth my tears, when I behold
    My country, e'en as Christ ('tis told)
Gazed weeping on Jerusalem.

When shall these longings be sufficed
    That stir my spirit night and day?
    When shall I see my country lay
Her homage at the Feet of Christ?

Here neither loss nor ruin is,
    Here death and ending hold no sway;
    In Christ is life beyond decay,
A treasure-store of purest bliss.

How thirst I for that blessed day
    When India's spiritual power
    And all her ancient wisdom's dower
Shall own His consummating sway!

Now soul and body, mind and will,
    Honour and name, my wealth, my all,
    Brethren and kindred, great and small,
I yield, Thy purpose to fulfil.

Of all I have, O Saviour sweet,
　All gifts, all skill, all thoughts of mind,
　A living garland I entwine
And offer at Thy lotus feet.

Christ, my soul's Rest, my Comrade true!
　Thine be my love through all my days;
　Let me not cease to sing Thy praise
In joyous verses ever new.

LOVE'S ECSTASY

Ah, love, I sink in the timeless sleep,
　Sink in the timeless sleep:
One Image stands before my eyes,
　And thrills my bosom's deep:
One vision bathes in radiant light
　My spirit's palace-halls;
All stir of hand, all throb of brain,
　Quivers, and sinks, and falls.
My soul fares forth; no fetters now
　Chain me to this world's shore.
Sleep! I would sleep! In pity spare;
　Let no man wake me more!

MY *TAI*

*(addressed to his own daughter; the
name means "sister" and would be
used in her own home)*

Tai, thou art my floweret bright,
My planet beauteous in the night;
Thou the jewel on my brow,
And my little birdie thou;
Yet thy grace how may I tell?
My sweetness doth all these excel!

Fair is the smiling of the rose,
But thine, strange mysteries doth disclose;
And opening rosebuds cannot show
Such sweetness as thy lips bestow.

All the planets of the night
Gleam but with a borrowed light;
But thou dost shine by thine own grace,
And shedd'st thy light in every place.

Jewels sparkle fair to see,
Yet how hard and cold they be!
And, how bright soe'er they shine,
Their beauty waxes not like thine.

Happy birdie all day long
Trills his many-splendoured song;
But th' angel choirs that make heaven ring
Dance with joy when thou dost sing!

THE TRANSFORMING PRESENCE

Be Thou at hand, O Lord;
Then, though this flesh reside
In stately palace halls
Or rugged mountain-side,
If Thine unfailing presence be
About me still, all's heaven to me.

Be Thou at hand, O Lord;
Then, though my board be piled
With wealth of daintiest fare
Or bitter herbs and wild,
The whiles my spirit trysts with Thee,
Thyself my nectar feast shall be.

Be Thou at hand, O Lord;
Then, though my nightly bed
On soft and fragrant flowers
Or roughest rocks be spread,
So but I lean upon Thy breast,
No breath of care shall mar my rest.

O dear and inmost soul
Of all the joys that be,
My action, thought and speech,
Yea all, I yield to Thee.
Lord Christ beloved, accept me now;
Unfailing Rest alone art Thou.

THE LAST VALLEY

O Brother, on my shoulder rests Thy hand,
    And fearless waits my soul;
O Way, erect on Thee I take my stand,
    And radiant gleams my goal;
O Truth, within the warmth of Thine embrace,
    All doubts dissolving die;
O Life, before the sunshine of Thy face,
    Death perisheth, not I!
Thy servant saith, Today there draweth near
    That latest valley—and wherefore should I fear?

FROM THE *CHRISTAYAN*
*(translated by Bishop Philip Loyd, retaining
the original Marathi Ovi metre)*

Whatever I have shed of tears
    For Mother India in past years
A woven garland now appears
    Laid, cleansed of fears At Thy blest feet.

And in the days to come, what more
    Of sorrow may yet be in store—
My Motherland and (though so poor)
    Myself I pour Into Thy hands.

As in the potter's hand the clay,
    So in Thy hand my mind to lay,
O Father, I am come this day;
    Take it, I pray For evermore.

HUSH THEE, HUSH THEE
(*translated by Dr. Nicol Macnicol*)

Hush Thee, hush Thee, baby Christ,
  Lord of all mankind;
Thou the happy lullaby
  Of my mind.

Hush Thee, hush Thee, Jesus, Lord,
  Stay of all Thou art;
Thou the happy lullaby
  Of my heart.

Hush Thee, hush Thee, Home of peace—
  Lo, Love lying there;
Thou the happy lullaby
  Of my care.

Hush Thee, hush Thee, Soul of mine,
  Setting all men free;
Thou the happy lullaby
  Of the whole of me.

PRAYER
(*translated by Dr. Nicol Macnicol*)

Prayer, to a heart of lowly love,
  Opens the gate of heaven above.

Ah, prayer is God's high dwelling place
  Wherein His children see His face.

From earth to heaven we build a stair—
  The name by which we call it, prayer.

Prayer is the gracious Father's knee;
  On it the child climbs lovingly.

Love's rain, the Spirit's holy ray,
  And tears of joy, are theirs who pray.

To walk with God, to feel His kiss,
  Yea, prayer, His servant owns, is this.

INSATIATE

The more I win Thee, Lord,
   the more for Thee I pine;
Ah, such a heart is mine!

My eyes behold Thee and
   are filled, and straightway then
Their hunger wakes again!

My arms have clasped Thee and
   should set Thee free, but no,
I cannot let Thee go!

Thou dwell'st within my heart;
   forthwith anew the fire
Burns of my soul's desire.

Lord Jesus Christ, Beloved,
   tell, O tell me true,
What shall Thy servant do?

GLOSSARY OF INDIAN WORDS

Ayah, children's nurse.

Bai, woman; often added as an honorific to a woman's first name, as

Rao is added to a man's first name.

Bajri and *Jowari*, grain used for making bread, sold by the

Seer, a measure of grain.

Haldi-kunku, the painting of a red spot on the forehead of every married and marriageable Hindu woman.

Kirtan, a story chanted to music, with choruses.

Munshi, a teacher of the Urdu language, as

Pandit is the Marathi word for teacher.

Ram, a favourite Hindu God.

Sari, the long cloth wound round as woman's clothing.

Sahib, Sir.

Supari, the betel nut producing a red juice, often wrapped in

Pan, a leaf, and a favourite chewing substance.

Tonga, a small horse-drawn carriage.